DINING IN

WESTPORT YOUNG WOMAN'S LEAGUE
WESTPORT, CONNECTICUT

COOKBOOK COMMITTEES

Cookbook Editor and Chairman, 1986-1987
Carole Rogers

Food Editors
Karen Greenbaum, Jan Jones, Liz Stokes

Planning Committee

Evi Allen	Nancy Hahnfeldt	Jean Neisius
Jean Bleyle	Ronnie Hittson	Sharon Schroeder
Katie Chase	Virginia Kress	Jeannette Tewey
Beverly Ellsley	Cia Marion	Michele Thain

General Committee

Pegi Bernard	Patti Graebner	Katie Nowlin
Pat Blaufuss	Mary Kneisel	Nancy Perrin
Elisabeth K. Boas	Eileen Knittel	Tammy Pincavage
Tanis Bond	Pat Markham	Kay Prybylski
Carol Carter	Alix Morin	Eva Rosenblatt
Mari Fleming	Debbie Murphy	

Development Chairmen, 1985–1986
Carla Cohn, Cindy Fitzgerald

Committee

Tanis Bond	Kaye Leong	Eva Rosenblatt
Mari Fleming	Maureen Luby	Marylea Schmidt
Connie Goodman	Pat Markham	Sharon Schroeder
Ronnie Hittson	Dorothy Rolla	Liz Stokes

Marketing Chairman, 1987-1988
Sharon Schroeder

Promotional Events

Creative Arts Festival	Kitchen and House Tour
Dorothy Rolla	Eva Rosenblatt, Pat Markham

The Westport Young Woman's League proudly presents DINING IN as a celebration of its thirtieth anniversary and of the town it serves.

Located along the banks of the Saugatuck River and the beaches of Long Island Sound some 50 miles east of New York City, Westport, Connecticut is a handsome New England town with a rich historical and cultural heritage dating from pre-Revolutionary times. The cannons at Compo Beach, the Minute Man statue nearby, numerous rustic homes, many stone fences and plentiful old trees remind us of our Colonial roots. Industrial buildings recall Westport's prominence in the nineteenth century when we were also known as the Union Army's major supplier of onions. The advent of the railroad diminished these roles yet helped shape the present identity of this town of commuters, executives, professionals, merchants, weekenders, artists, and writers.

As early as 1910, trainloads of New Yorkers headed for Westport's beaches and country life. Our present reputation as a haven for artists, writers, cartoonists, thespians (and now, by extension, advertising, radio and television people) dates from the turn of the century. To this day Westport boasts an unusual amount of artistic activity, including two nationally recognized summer stock playhouses and an outdoor concerts-in-the-park pavilion.

In its thirty years, the Westport Young Woman's League, a nonprofit, educational, service, and social organization, has raised more than $500,000 to help preserve the quality of life in Westport and the surrounding towns. We continue to provide educational programs and volunteers for the schools and other youth-oriented groups; and to create, fund, and staff projects for people of all ages and needs. Fundraisers, including the Creative Arts (Crafts) Festival, Minute Man Road Race, House Tour, and DINING IN itself, generate the proceeds of which members are so proud. League members have held leadership roles in many of the nonprofit organizations in the area and the League itself has contributed many hours of service and direct funding for these and other worthy causes.

Through service and the rewards it brings us, many lasting friendships have grown and been nourished by the role that cooking and dining play in League activities and individual lives. We have included some old family favorites, some new discoveries, and other recipes long-used by our members. If all of these offer a peek into the culinary lives of League members, then we hope that the photographs create a glimpse of the traditions and lifestyles of Westport. We thank all the members, celebrities, restaurateurs, creative professionals and friends who have contributed to DINING IN. We invite you to share in the varied tastes of Westport and the Westport Young Woman's League.

Carole Rogers, Cookbook Editor
Nancy S. Hahnfeldt, President 1985-86
Veronnie H. Hittson, President 1986-87
Mimi Greenlee, President 1987-88

Editor
CAROLE ROGERS

Drawings
MELANIE BELL

Styling
REBECCA NEWMAN

Photography
SETH GOLTZER

Laser Typesetting
NANCY HAHNFELDT

Consultant
MIGGS BURROUGHS

Special thanks to:

Champion International Paper Company
Westport Word Works
Dr. and Mrs. Richard Boas
Mr. and Mrs. John Carter
Mr. and Mrs. Stan Drake
Beverly Ellsley
Fairfield County Model A Club
Mr. and Mrs. Clark Graebner
Mr. and Mrs. John Hittson
Mr. and Mrs. Barry Knittel
Mr. and Mrs. Carmine Picarello
Mr. Louis Rogers
Martha Stewart
Joanne Woodward
Le Chambord
La Clé d'Or
Dameon's
Il Villano
Pompano Grille
Sakura of Westport

TABLE OF CONTENTS

Proceeds from the sale of DINING IN will be contributed to community organizations by the Westport Young Woman's League. Past recipients include:

A Wish Come True
The Alcoholism and Drug
    Dependency Council
American Cancer Society
American Red Cross
Burn Center of Bridgeport
C.L.A.S.P. and C.L.A.S.P. Homes
CACLD CT
Camp Hemlock
Camp Sunrise
Candlelighters
CES Marine Biology Course
Child Care Council of Westport-
    Weston
Community Council of Westport-
    Weston
C.O.P.E.
CT Society to Prevent Blindness
Department of Human Services
Elderhouse
Family & Children's Aid, Greater
    Norwalk
Firemen's Benevolent Fund
FISH of Westport
Girl Scouts
Helping Hands
The Hole in the Wall Gang
I Can Do It Too
Interfaith Housing Assoc. of
    Westport-Weston
Juvenile Diabetes Foundation
Keystone House
Kids on the Block
Levitt Pavilion for the Performing
    Arts
Literacy Volunteers of Greater
    Norwalk
Lockwood Mathews Mansion
Maritime Center of Norwalk
Meals on Wheels
Michael Kowall Memorial Fund
Mid-Fairfield Child Guidance
Mid-Fairfield Hospice
Mohonk House
Music Found. for Handicapped of CT

Nature Center—NCEA
Norwalk Hospital
Odyssey of the Mind Association
Officer Friendly Program
PAL
Pegasus
Performers of Connecticut
Project Renaissance
Project Return
Retired Senior Volunteer Program,
    R.S.V.P.
Saugatuck Day Care Service
Save the Children
Special Olympics
Staples Band Uniforms
Staples High School Scholarship
    Fund
Staples Orphenians
Students Against Drunken Driving
Susan Lloyd Educational Memorial
    Fund
STAR
United Cerebral Palsy
Visiting Homemaker Service
Vitam Center
WECAN
Westport Arts Center
Westport Historical Society
Westport Little League
Westport PTA Cultural Arts
    Committee
Westport Public Library—
    Book–a–Baby
Westport Public Library, Youth
    Service
Westport Regional Center,
    Coleytown
Westport Senior Center
Westport VEMS
Westport-Weston Counseling
    Service
Westport Woman's Club
Women's Crisis Center
Women Helping Women
YMCA

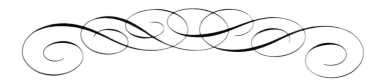

Appetizers

Eggplant with Pine Nuts

1 medium eggplant (1-1 1/2
  pounds)
3/4 cup olive oil, approximately
10 cherry tomatoes
1 clove garlic, finely minced
1 tablespoon finely chopped onion

1/2 cup pine nuts
salt and pepper to taste
1/4 cup finely chopped fresh
  parsley
lemon wedges for garnish
pita bread

Trim the ends of the eggplant and cut into 1/4-inch thick slices.

In a saucepan heat 1/4 cup of the oil and cook the eggplant until golden brown on both sides, adding more oil as necessary. Drain the slices on paper towels. Chop the eggplant and place in a mixing bowl.

Meanwhile, drop the cherry tomatoes into boiling water and let stand about 5 seconds. Drain immediately. Peel the tomatoes. Chop and add them to the eggplant mixture. Add the garlic, onion and pine nuts. Season to taste with salt and pepper. Transfer to a serving bowl. Cover and refrigerate for four hours.

Bring to room temperature before serving and sprinkle with the parsley. Garnish with the lemon wedges.

Serve with pita bread.

Zucchini Mini-Quiches

3 cups zucchini, thinly sliced
1 cup Bisquick
1/2 cup chopped onion
1/4 teaspoon seasoned salt
1/2 cup vegetable oil
1/2 cup grated Parmesan cheese

2 tablespoons finely chopped
  fresh parsley
1/2 teaspoon dried marjoram or
  oregano
1 large clove garlic, minced
4 eggs, lightly beaten
black pepper to taste

Preheat oven to 350°. Butter 48 miniature muffin tins.

In a bowl mix all the ingredients thoroughly and fill tins. Bake until browned, about 20 to 25 minutes. Serve hot.

Tapenade Canapés

4 to 6 anchovy fillets soaked in
  water for 10 minutes
1 pound black olives, cured in oil,
  pitted
1 clove garlic
a 7-ounce can tuna in olive oil,
  drained

2 tablespoons capers
3 tablespoons olive oil
juice of 1 lemon
1 teaspoon black pepper
12 thin slices white bread, crusts
  removed
24 oil-cured olives for garnish

In a food processor puree the anchovies, the 1 pound of olives, garlic, tuna, capers, olive oil, lemon juice and pepper. *Can be made a day in advance up to this point.*

Cut each slice of bread into four triangles and spread each with about 2 teaspoons of the tapenade. Garnish with half an olive.

The canapés may be made an hour before serving but do not refrigerate them.

48 canapés

Red Caviar with Crème Fraîche

a 4-ounce jar red caviar
1 cup crème fraîche

2 scallions, minced
thinly sliced black bread

Arrange caviar in a mound in center of a serving plate. Spoon crème fraîche around base of mound. Make a border around the caviar and crème fraîche with the scallions. Arrange bread around rim of plate.

Crème fraîche must be prepared a day in advance.

Crème Fraîche
1 cup heavy cream
  (not ultrapasteurized)

1 tablespoon sour cream

In a small saucepan combine the heavy cream and sour cream. Whisk over low heat until lukewarm (85°). Transfer to a glass jar and cover loosely. Let stand at room temperature until thickened, 12 to 24 hours. Stir well. Cover and refrigerate.

Chili Cheese Squares

three 4-ounce cans diced green
  chilies, drained
1 pound Monterey Jack cheese,
  grated

4 eggs
a 5-ounce can evaporated milk
salt and pepper to taste

Preheat oven to 350°. Oil a 9x12-inch jelly-roll pan.

Spread the chilies evenly over the bottom of the prepared pan. Sprinkle the Monterey Jack cheese evenly over the chilies.

In a bowl beat the eggs with the milk, adding salt and pepper to taste. Pour evenly over cheese. Bake for 30 minutes or until cheese is lightly browned. Cool and cut into bite-size pieces.

Serve hot or at room temperature.

Can be made in advance and reheated.

Chicken Satay

1 pound chicken breasts, boned
2 tablespoons brown sugar
2 tablespoons soy sauce
2 teaspoons curry powder
1 teaspoon red wine vinegar
1 tablespoon vegetable oil

3 tablespoons peanut butter
2 tablespoons sherry
2 cloves garlic, minced
dash of Tabasco sauce
wooden skewers soaked in cold
  water

Cut chicken into 1-inch chunks.

In a bowl combine all the ingredients except the chicken. Add the chicken chunks and marinate at least two hours.

Preheat broiler or prepare barbecue grill.

Thread chicken chunks onto skewers and quickly broil 4 to 7 inches from heat.

Mussels in Cream Sauce

4 pounds mussels scrubbed clean or two 10-ounce packages frozen mussels	1 teaspoon curry powder
	3 tablespoons unsalted butter
	3 tablespoons flour
1 cup dry white wine	1 cup heavy cream
5 shallots, chopped	salt and white pepper to taste
2 cloves garlic, crushed	minced parsley

In a deep pot add the wine, shallots and garlic and bring to a boil. Add the mussels, cover and steam over high heat, shaking the pot occasionally, until the mussels have opened. Discard any that do not open.

Remove the mussels and reserve the liquid. Strain the liquid through a cheesecloth to remove all the sand. Transfer to a saucepan, add the curry and bring to a boil.

Knead the butter and flour with the fingertips and drop into the boiling liquid, stirring continuously with a whisk. Remove from heat, slowly add the cream and return saucepan to the heat. Cook until the sauce is thickened and coats the back of a wooden spoon.

Correct seasoning with salt and pepper.

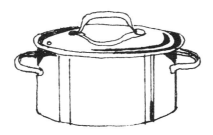

To serve:

Discard top shells leaving mussels in bottom shells. Arrange on salad greens. Pour sauce over the mussels and sprinkle with the parsley.

Or, discard the shells and stir the mussels into the sauce. Serve in baked puff pastry shells.

$\mathcal{S}$tuffed Cherry Tomatoes or Snow Peas

24 Cherry Tomatoes

Core and remove pulp and seeds from tomatoes with a small melon ball cutter. Turn upside down on paper towels and drain for 30 minutes.
Can be filled and refrigerated up to four hours in advance.

48 Fresh Snow Peas

Split peas two-thirds down one side. Blanch in lightly salted boiling water for 10 seconds. Remove and immediately plunge into cold water. Drain well.
Can be filled and refrigerated up to three hours in advance.

Salmon Cream Cheese Filling

4 ounces Nova Scotia smoked salmon, chopped
a 3-ounce package cream cheese, softened
1/4 teaspoon Worcestershire sauce
l teaspoon finely chopped fresh chives

In a food processor mix thoroughly the salmon, cream cheese, Worcestershire sauce and chives.

Crab Filling

1 1/2 cups (12 ounces) crabmeat
1/2 cup mayonnaise
1 large shallot, minced
1 teaspoon Worcestershire sauce
1/2 cup finely chopped celery
1 teaspoon capers

In a bowl combine all the ingredients and blend thoroughly.

Chicken Tarragon Filling

1 large chicken breast, poached, boned and cut into pieces
1/4 cup almonds
4 ounces cream cheese, softened
1/2 teaspoon dried tarragon
salt and pepper to taste

In a food processor coarsely grind the almonds. Remove and set aside.
In the same bowl process the chicken briefly. Add the almonds, cream cheese and tarragon and blend well. Adjust seasoning with salt and pepper.

12

Herb Egg Filling

4 hard-cooked eggs, sieved
3 tablespoons mayonnaise
1 tablespoon Dijon mustard
1 tablespoon minced scallion

1 tablespoon of minced fresh
parsley, chives, dill, basil or
tarragon
salt and pepper to taste

In a bowl combine all the ingredients and blend thoroughly. Adjust seasoning with salt and pepper.

Smoked Salmon Torte

two 8-ounce packages cream
cheese, softened
1 cup (2 sticks) unsalted butter,
softened
1 tablespoon grated lemon rind
1 tablespoon lemon juice

1/2 cup finely chopped fresh dill
1/4 pound smoked salmon, finely
chopped
1/2 cup red lumpfish caviar
sprigs of fresh dill
vegetables and crackers

In a small bowl beat together the cream cheese and butter until light and fluffy. Add the lemon rind and juice. Divide mixture into thirds: place one-third in a bowl, and the other two-thirds in a second bowl. Mix chopped dill into the one-third until well blended. Blend chopped salmon into the other two-thirds.

Line a 2 1/2 cup bowl with plastic wrap leaving a 2-inch overhang.

Firmly pack salmon-cheese mixture into lined bowl. Spread 1/4 cup of the caviar evenly over salmon mixture.

Carefully spread dill-cheese mixture over caviar and pack firmly. Cover with plastic wrap overhang. Refrigerate until firm, about two to three hours. Remove 1/2 hour before serving.

To serve:

Fold back plastic wrap. Unmold onto serving platter. Carefully remove plastic wrap. Garnish top of torte with remaining caviar and dill sprigs.

Serve with snow peas, zucchini rounds and endive for dipping or flatbread and crackers for spreading.

Lamb and Curry Won Ton

3/4 pound ground lamb
2 tablespoons unsalted butter
3 cups minced onion
1 teaspoon minced garlic
1 teaspoon minced fresh ginger
1 tablespoon fresh lemon juice
1/2 teaspoon salt

1/2 cup hot water
1 teaspoon dried mint
1 tablespoon chopped fresh
  parsley
1 tablespoon curry powder
80 to 90 3 1/2-inch won ton
  wrappers
melted butter

Preheat oven to 425°. Position rack in upper third of oven.

In a large saucepan melt the butter and sauté 1 1/2 cups of the onion, the garlic and ginger and cook until onion is softened. Blend in the lemon juice and salt. Increase heat to high, add the lamb and sauté until meat is no longer pink. Stir in the water.

Lower heat, cover and simmer until lamb is still moist but not watery, about 15 minutes, stirring frequently during end of cooking to prevent burning. (The meat mixture should be fairly dry or the moisture will prevent the won tons from getting crisp.) Stir in the mint, parsley, curry powder and remaining 1 1/2 cups onion. Cover and cook 2 minutes. Let cool.

Fill each wrapper with 1 slightly rounded teaspoon of filling. Flatten slightly, then fold over, egg roll style. *Can be made in advance up to this point.*

Arrange on ungreased baking sheets. Brush lightly with butter. Bake until golden brown, about 15 minutes. Serve with Apricot or Plum Sauce.

Apricot Sauce
1 generous tablespoon dry mustard
1 teaspoon (or more) water

peanut oil
a 12-ounce jar apricot preserves

In a small bowl mix the mustard with enough water to form a smooth paste. Blend in several drops of peanut oil.

In a food processor puree the preserves until smooth. Transfer to a bowl and combine with the mustard mixture. Thin with small amount of water, if necessary.

Cover and refrigerate. Serve chilled. *Can be prepared a day in advance.*

Plum Sauce
1/4 cup plum preserves
1 tablespoon cider vinegar
1 tablespoon water
1 teaspoon grated orange rind

1/2 teaspoon cornstarch
1/2 teaspoon soy sauce
1/4 teaspoon dry mustard

In a processor combine together all the ingredients. Transfer to a small saucepan. Bring to a boil, stirring constantly. Remove from heat and let cool. Cover and refrigerate. Serve chilled. *Can be prepared a day in advance.*

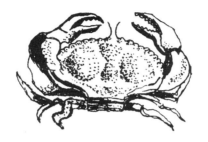

$\mathcal{S}$hrimp and Scallop Seviche

2 pounds shrimp, cooked,
   deveined and cut into thirds
1 pound raw bay scallops
1 cup lime juice (about 6 limes)
6 tablespoons finely chopped red
   onion
4 tablespoons chopped fresh
   parsley

2 tablespoons finely chopped
   green pepper
1/2 cup olive oil
1/2 teaspoon dried oregano
dash of Tabasco sauce
salt and pepper to taste

In a bowl mix together the shrimp and scallops. Add the lime juice, cover and marinate for one hour at room temperature, stirring occasionally.

Drain and discard the juice. In a bowl combine the seafood with the remaining ingredients. Cover and refrigerate for one hour.

A FAMILY DINNER

Westport is home to many celebrities in the theater and the arts. Some are particularly treasured, not just for their accomplishments, but for the active role they take in helping to keep Westport unique. None is more dedicated than actress/director Joanne Woodward who, along with husband Paul Newman, has made Westport her home. One of Ms. Woodward's special interests has been the restoration and preservation of Wheeler House, the site of the Westport Historical Society. Just as she has treasured Wheeler House's historical significance, so too Joanne Woodward treasures the family china and crystal she provided for this picture, taken at Wheeler House. Through the years, the League and its members have continued to support the work of the Westport Historical Society in preserving the history of our town.

Chicken Liver Terrine

2 slices (3 ounces) French bread,
  crusts removed
1/2 cup chicken broth
8 tablespoons (1 stick) unsalted
  butter
1 pound chicken livers, cut in half
3 cloves garlic, finely chopped
1 medium onion, finely chopped

1/4 pound mushrooms, chopped
2 tablespoons cognac
3 eggs, lightly beaten
1/2 cup heavy cream
1/8 teaspoon pepper
1/2 teaspoon thyme
2 teaspoons salt
cornichons and dill bread

Must be prepared a day in advance.

Preheat oven to 350°. Butter a 1-quart terrine.

Soak bread in chicken broth and set aside.
In a large saucepan heat the butter and sauté the livers until firm but still pink inside. Remove livers and set aside.
To the same saucepan add the garlic and onion and sauté until onion is very soft. Add the mushrooms and sauté until mushrooms have released their liquid. Set pan aside.
Crumble the bread (it should have absorbed all the broth) and place in a food processor. Add the cognac and blend with 2 to 3 on/off turns. Add the livers and blend only until well combined. *Do not puree.* Mixture will be slightly lumpy.
In a large bowl combine the eggs, cream, spices and onion and mushroom mixture. Add the liver mixture and combine until well mixed. Pour mixture into the terrine. Cover tightly with foil and bake in a bain marie for 1 hour or until the center is firm to the touch. Remove and let cool.
Refrigerate overnight to mellow the flavors and firm texture.
Serve from terrine with cornichons and sliced dill bread.

*O*ven Barbecued Chicken Wings

5 pounds chicken wings
3 teaspoons paprika
1/2 cup vegetable oil
2 teaspoons pepper
1 cup ketchup
1/4 cup honey
3 tablespoons red vinegar
3 tablespoons white vinegar

2 tablespoons Worcestershire
  sauce
1 teaspoon Tabasco sauce
1 tablespoon Dijon mustard
1 clove garlic, crushed
4 tablespoons (1/2 stick) unsalted
  butter
1 bay leaf

Preheat oven to 400°.

Sprinkle chicken wings with 2 teaspoons of the paprika and 1/4 cup of the oil. Turn wings to coat. Place in a large roasting pan and bake 15 minutes.

In a saucepan combine the remaining ingredients and bring to a boil. Baste both sides of the chicken wings several times until the wings have cooked, about 1 hour.

# *S*teak Tartare

Contributed by Owner–Chef, Horst Antosch,
La Clé d'Or, Westport

1 1/2 pounds freshly ground flank
  steak or round steak, well
  trimmed*
2 anchovy fillets, mashed
1/2 teaspoon capers
1 egg yolk
3 drops Tabasco sauce
2 dashes Worcestershire sauce

1/2 teaspoon paprika
1 tablespoon chopped sour pickles
2 tablespoons chopped onions
salt and pepper to taste
cornichons and radishes for
  garnish
bread and unsalted butter

In a bowl combine all the ingredients until just blended. Transfer to a serving platter. Garnish with the cornichons and radishes.

Serve immediately with rye or whole grain bread and butter.

*Have the butcher grind the meat or chop in a food processor, being careful not to overprocess.

lazed Brie

an 8-inch wheel Brie cheese
1/3 cup almonds
1/3 cup walnuts
1/4 teaspoon cinnamon
pinch each of nutmeg and allspice

1/2 cup light brown sugar
1-3 tablespoons water
dried apricots, fruit and crackers

In a food processor finely grind together the almonds, walnuts, cinnamon, nutmeg, allspice and sugar. Add 1 tablespoon of water and process. If the mixture does not hold together, add another tablespoon of water. It should be moist but not runny. Spread the mixture on the Brie cheese.

Preheat broiler.

Place the Brie under the broiler but watch it constantly. Broil until the topping is lightly browned and sugar has caramelized.

Serve with the apricots, fruit and crackers.

aked Brie

a 6-inch wheel Brie cheese
1 frozen puff pastry sheet,
  thawed

1 egg yolk, beaten
crackers and fruit

Preheat oven to 450°.

Roll out the pastry sheet. With the empty Brie container cut out one circle, same size. Cut another circle, larger than the Brie. Place Brie on this circle and fold up the sides. Place first circle on top. Cut strips of pastry 1/2 inch wide and wrap around top edges. Crimp to join the top crust and folded-up sides. Brush with the egg yolk. *Can be frozen up to this point.*

Bake for 10 minutes, lower heat to 350° and continue to bake until crust is lightly browned, about 20 minutes.

Serve with crackers and fruit.

$\mathscr{S}$tuffed Mushrooms

Mushroom Filling

2 1/2 pounds fresh medium
  mushrooms
8 tablespoons (1 stick) unsalted
  butter
1 large onion, finely chopped
3 cloves garlic, minced

1 bay leaf
1/4 cup red wine
3 tablespoons finely chopped
  fresh parsley
salt and pepper to taste
fresh bread crumbs

Preheat oven to 350°.

Carefully separate the stems from the mushroom caps. Place caps on a baking sheet. Finely chop the stems and set aside.

In a large saucepan melt the butter and sauté the onion and garlic until the onion is soft and golden. Add the bay leaf, wine, parsley, mushroom stems and cook, stirring occasionally, for 5 minutes.

Add salt and pepper and enough bread crumbs to form a stuffing consistency. Remove bay leaf and stuff mushroom caps. Bake for 30 minutes.

Ham Filling

1 pound fresh mushrooms
2 tablespoons olive oil
1/4 cup minced onion
1 clove garlic, minced
5 ounces chopped ham
2 tablespoons grated Parmesan
  cheese

1 egg, lightly beaten
2 tablespoons chopped fresh
  parsley
1/2 teaspoon dried oregano
1/2 teaspoon salt
pepper to taste
dry bread crumbs

Carefully separate the stems from the mushroom caps. Place caps on a baking sheet. Finely chop enough mushroom stems to make 1/2 cup, reserving the rest for another use.

In a saucepan heat the oil and sauté the chopped mushroom stems, onion and garlic. Cook until mixture is very soft, about 10 minutes. Remove from heat and stir in the ham, cheese, egg, parsley, oregano and salt and pepper. Add enough bread crumbs to form a stuffing consistency. If mixture seems too dry, add a teaspoon of olive oil.

Stuff mushroom caps. Bake for 30 minutes.

ravlax

a 4-pound center section of
    salmon, filleted but with skin
    left intact
4 large bunches dill
3 tablespoons kosher salt

3 tablespoons white peppercorns,
    coarsely crushed
4 tablespoons sugar
Mustard Sauce
pumpernickel bread

Must be prepared four to five days in advance.

The salmon, dill and spices are combined in alternating layers. Divide dill into two bunches. Layer one bunch on the bottom of a deep glass dish, large enough to hold one salmon fillet. Place one fillet, skin side down on top of the dill.

In a small bowl blend the salt, peppercorns and sugar. Sprinkle and pat half of the mixture onto the fillet. Cover with the second bunch of dill. Rub the remaining salt mixture on the other fillet and place on top of the dill, skin side up. Cover the salmon with plastic wrap and place a 14-ounce can or other weight on top. Refrigerate, weighted, for at least four days.

Each day, remove the weights and carefully turn over both fillets, sandwich style, leaving the bottom layer of dill. Spoon some of the liquids that accumulated in the dish between and on top of the fillets. Cover again, replace weights and return to the refrigerator.

Before serving, scrape away the dill and salt mixture. Reserve the dill and 5 tablespoons of the marinade for the Mustard Sauce. Place the fillets skin side down on a cutting board and carve the fillets diagonally into very thin slices.

Serve with Mustard Sauce and thinly sliced pumpernickel bread.

Mustard Sauce

1/4 cup Dijon mustard
1/4 cup spicy brown mustard
3 tablespoons sugar
3 tablespoons white vinegar
5 tablespoons of salmon marinade
2 tablespoons cognac

salt and pepper to taste
3/4 cup peanut oil
1/2 cup chopped fresh dill
1/2 cup chopped dill from the
    marinade, stems removed

In a bowl mix all the ingredients except the oil and dill. Beat the mixture with a whisk and slowly add the oil in a steady stream. Stir in the dill. Transfer to a serving bowl.

ortilla Roll-ups

an 8-ounce package cream cheese,
    softened
a 4-ounce can green chilies,
    drained and chopped

2 scallions, minced
dash of garlic powder
5 large flour tortillas

In a bowl combine all the ingredients except the tortillas and mix well.

Spread 1 heaping teaspoon onto each tortilla and roll up jelly-roll fashion. Place tortillas seam side down on a baking sheet, cover and refrigerate two hours. Slice rolls into bite-size pieces.

Serve with Hot Picante Sauce.

Hot Picante Sauce
1 onion, finely chopped
1 bunch scallions, chopped
2-3 cloves garlic, minced
1 fresh jalapeño pepper or
a 4-ounce can jalapeños, drained,
    seeded and chopped

1 tablespoon minced coriander
3 tomatoes, finely chopped
1/2 small green or red pepper
1 tablespoon lemon juice
salt to taste

If using fresh jalapeño, remove seeds with rubber gloves.

In a bowl combine all the ingredients. Cover and refrigerate several hours, preferably overnight.

48 servings

egetable Terrine

Contributed by Chef Robert Pouget, Le Chambord, Westport

10 ounces small green beans
10 ounces butternut squash, cut
   into 1/4-inch thick slices
10 ounces baby carrots
3 small avocados, ripe but firm
1/2 lemon
1 pound boned chicken breast,
   diced
juice of 1 lemon

1/2 cup chopped fresh parsley
salt and pepper to taste
2 egg whites
1 cup corn oil
a 16-ounce jar grape leaves,
   drained, rinsed and patted dry,
   or 15-20 fresh grape leaves,
   blanched

Must be prepared a day in advance. Every ingredient must be very cold and as dry as possible before assembling. Place food processor in freezer until ready to use.

In a pot of salted boiling water cook separately the green beans, butternut squash and carrots until crisp tender. Drain and refresh each vegetable in ice water. Drain well, wrap in a towel and refrigerate.

Cut the avocados in half. Rub with 1/2 lemon and refrigerate. In the chilled food processor blend the diced chicken, lemon juice, parsley and salt and pepper. Add the egg whites and blend well. Slowly pour the oil in a steady stream. Return the food processor to the refrigerator.

Line a 9x5x3-inch pan with the grape leaves, rib side in. Overlap the leaves slightly and allow to extend over edge of pan. Spread a thin layer of the chicken mixture. Arrange the carrots on top, lengthwise. Alternate layers of the mixture with the green beans, squash and avocado halves, cut side up. Finish with a thin layer of the mixture. Wrap the vine leaves over the top and cover with a sheet of buttered wax paper.

Preheat oven to 375°.

Set the terrine in a pan of boiling water and bake for 30 minutes. Cool the terrine and refrigerate overnight.
Serve with Horseradish Sauce.

Horseradish Sauce

1 tablespoon unsalted butter
1 tablespoon flour
1/4 cup chicken broth
1/4 cup milk
1/4 cup heavy cream

dash of nutmeg
1 tablespoon bottled horseradish,
  drained or to taste
salt and pepper to taste

In a saucepan melt the butter and add the flour, stirring with a wire whisk. Add the chicken broth and milk, whisking continuously, until thickened and smooth. Gradually mix in the cream and nutmeg. Stir in the horseradish and adjust seasoning with salt and pepper.

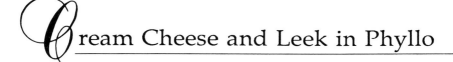ream Cheese and Leek in Phyllo

1 leek, including green top, well
  washed and thinly sliced
4 tablespoons (1/2 stick) unsalted
  butter
an 8-ounce package cream cheese,
  softened

2 egg yolks, lightly beaten
1 tablespoon minced fresh dill
scant 1/4 teaspoon salt
dash of black pepper
8 phyllo dough sheets
melted butter

Preheat oven to 350°.

In a saucepan melt the butter and sauté the leek until soft, about 20 minutes. Transfer to a bowl and combine with the remaining ingredients except the phyllo sheets and melted butter. Cover and chill.

To assemble:
  Keep phyllo dough covered with a damp towel while working.
  Brush one phyllo sheet with the butter and cut into 6 sections. Place 2 tablespoons of the leek filling on each section and fold egg roll style or in triangle fashion. *Can be frozen at this point.*
  Bake until crisp and golden, about 15 minutes.
  Serve immediately.

Cheese Calzones

two 1-pound packages puff pastry
  sheets, thawed
1 pound mozzarella cheese,
  grated
1/2 pound feta cheese
1/4 pound prosciutto ham, sliced
1/2 cup ricotta cheese
1/2 cup Parmesan cheese, grated

1 teaspoon dried rosemary
4 tablespoons finely chopped
  fresh parsley
4 tablespoons finely chopped
  chives
2 teaspoons minced garlic
4 teaspoons dried basil
black pepper to taste

Preheat oven to 350°.

In a large bowl crumble the feta cheese and add the mozzarella cheese. Cut the prosciutto ham into very thin strips and add to the cheese mixture. Stir in the ricotta and Parmesan cheeses. Add the herbs and spices and blend thoroughly.

To assemble:
Divide each pastry sheet into nine 4-inch squares.
Spoon 1 1/2 to 2 teaspoons of the cheese mixture into the center of each square. Moisten edges with cold water. Fold pastry over to form a triangle and crimp edges firmly together with a fork to seal securely. *Can be frozen at this point.*
Arrange calzones on baking sheets. Bake until golden, about 20 to 30 minutes.

ushroom Croustades

Croustades

24 slices fresh, thin sliced white bread

2 tablespoons very soft butter

Mushroom Filling

4 tablespoons (1/2 stick) unsalted butter

3 tablespoons finely chopped shallots

1/2 pound mushrooms, finely chopped

2 tablespoons flour

1 cup heavy cream

1/2 teaspoon salt

1/8 teaspoon red pepper

1 tablespoon finely chopped fresh parsley

1 1/2 tablespoons finely chopped fresh chives

1/2 teaspoon lemon juice

2 tablespoons grated Parmesan cheese

butter

Preheat oven to 400°.

Heavily butter 24 miniature muffin tins with the 2 tablespoons butter.

Cut a 3-inch round from each slice of bread. Carefully fit each into the muffin tins to form a cup. Bake for 10 minutes.

Remove from tins and cool. Reduce oven temperature to 350°.

In a heavy saucepan melt the 4 tablespoons butter. Add the shallots and cook for 4 minutes. Add the mushrooms and cook 10 to 15 minutes, stirring occasionally.

Sprinkle flour over mushroom mixture and stir until all traces of the flour disappear. Pour in the cream and, stirring constantly, bring mixture to a boil and cook 2 minutes. Remove from heat and stir in salt, cayenne, parsley, chives and lemon juice. Adjust seasoning, if necessary. Cool.

To assemble:

With a small spoon fill the croustades. Sprinkle lightly with the Parmesan cheese and dot with the butter.

Arrange on a baking sheet and bake for 10 minutes.

Can be frozen and reheated.

Marinated Shrimp

2 pounds medium shrimp,
deveined and cooked
1 pound carrots, cut into 1 1/4x2-
inch lengths

1 bunch celery, cut into 1 1/4x2-
inch lengths
3 medium onions, thinly sliced
1 clove garlic, cut in half
Marinade

Must be prepared a day in advance or longer.

Place half of the carrot sticks and celery sticks, onions and garlic in the bottom of a deep glass serving bowl. Add half of the shrimp. Pour in half of the Marinade. Repeat layers. Cover bowl and refrigerate overnight, preferably longer.

Marinade
8 bay leaves
3/4 cup vegetable oil
1 1/2 cups white vinegar
a 3 1/2-ounce jar capers with juice

2 teaspoons celery seed
1 1/2 teaspoons salt
dash of Tabasco sauce

Combine all the ingredients and blend thoroughly.

Baked Savory Loaf

1 dark rye bread loaf
an 8-ounce and a 3-ounce package
cream cheese, softened
1 pint sour cream
1 1/2 cups mayonnaise

5 ounces corned beef, chopped
4 scallions, chopped
3 ounces chopped Swiss cheese
1 teaspoon garlic powder

Preheat oven to 350°.

Hollow out the bread and reserve the inside pieces. In a bowl combine all the ingredients except the bread. Fill the bread shell, cover with foil and bake for about 50 minutes.

Serve hot with the reserved bread, cut into squares.

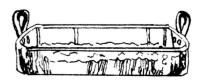

nchovy Cheese Roll-Ups

2 loaves thin sliced *soft* white
  bread, crusts removed
8 tablespoons (1 stick) unsalted
  butter, melted
1 tablespoon grated onion
dash of Tabasco sauce

1 teaspoon ketchup
1 teaspoon Worcestershire sauce
juice of 1/2 lemon
an 8-ounce package cream cheese,
  softened
3 ounces anchovy paste or to taste

Do not use a firm textured bread as it will not roll up properly.

Preheat broiler.

In a bowl mix together the onion, Tabasco sauce, ketchup, Worcestershire sauce, lemon juice, cream cheese and anchovy paste.

Roll each slice of bread very thinly with a rolling pin. Brush butter on one side of each slice. Spread with anchovy mixture and roll up. Brush top with butter. Broil until top is browned. Cut into serving pieces.

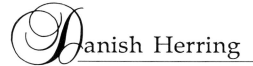anish Herring

a 13-ounce jar of herring tidbits
  poached in wine, drained and
  cut into bite-size pieces
1 cup mild tarragon vinegar
2/3 cup sugar
a 6-ounce can tomato paste

8 whole cloves
8 white peppercorns
4 bay leaves
1/2 cup chopped gerkins
1/2 cup chopped onions
rye bread

Must be prepared three days in advance.

In a small bowl combine all the ingredients except the herring. Add the herring and mix thoroughly. Cover and refrigerate for at least 3 days, turning occasionally.

Serve with thin slices of rye bread.

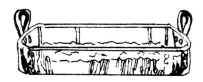

$\mathscr{S}$almon Mousse

2 envelopes plain gelatin
1/2 cup water
an 8-ounce can tomato sauce
2 teaspoons lemon juice
two 3- ounce packages cream
   cheese, softened
1/2 teaspoon chili powder
1 cup mayonnaise
1/2 cup finely chopped celery

2 teaspoons grated onion
1 scallion, finely chopped
1 tablespoon finely chopped fresh
   dill
two 8-ounce cans of red salmon,
   skinned, boned and drained
few drops Tabasco sauce
crackers and bread

Must be prepared a day in advance.

Lightly oil a 6-cup mold.
Dissolve the gelatin in 1/4 cup of water and set aside.
In a saucepan heat the remaining 1/4 cup of water with the tomato sauce and lemon juice. Bring to a boil. Remove from heat and stir in the gelatin. Set aside for 10 minutes.
In a food processor blend the cream cheese until smooth. Gradually add the tomato mixture and process until just combined. Add the remaining ingredients and mix briefly.
Pour salmon mixture into prepared mold and refrigerate overnight.
Serve with stoned wheat crackers and thinly sliced pumpernickel bread.

Mushroom Turnovers

8 tablespoons (1 stick) unsalted
   butter, softened
4 ounces cream cheese, softened
1 cup flour
1/2 pound mushrooms
2 tablespoons unsalted butter
1 small onion
1-2 tablespoons flour

2 -3 tablespoons chopped fresh
   parsley
1/4 cup dry sherry
1/4-1/2 teaspoon dried oregano
pepper to taste
1 egg, beaten with 1 teaspoon
   water for glaze

Preheat oven to 425°.

Dough

In a food processor, combine the butter, cream cheese and 1 cup flour and blend thoroughly. Transfer to a bowl, cover and refrigerate 1 hour.

Chop the mushrooms and onion in the food processor.

In a saucepan melt the butter and sauté the onions with the mushrooms until liquid evaporates. Sprinkle with the flour and mix well. Add the parsley, sherry, oregano and pepper. Remove from heat.

To assemble:

Divide dough in half and roll out paper thin. Cut circles out with a 3-inch scalloped cutter. Spoon a small amount of the mushroom mixture on each circle, off center. Moisten edges with water, fold in half and press with fingertips to seal edges. Crimp with a fork. *Can be frozen at this point.* Place in one layer on ungreased baking sheet.

Refrigerate 1/2 hour. Glaze turnovers with egg mixture. Bake until lightly browned, about 10 to 15 minutes. Serve immediately.

60 turnovers

Gorgonzola Cheese and Ham Spirals

2 puff pastry sheets, thawed
2/3 pound Gorgonzola cheese,
   well chilled

2 tablespoons plus 1 1/2 teaspoons
   dry sherry
1/3 pound ham, sliced paper thin
2 egg whites, beaten

In a mixer bowl beat the Gorgonzola cheese until light. Mix in the sherry.

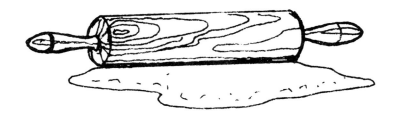

Roll out 1 pastry sheet to a 10x12-inch rectangle. Spread half of the cheese mixture evenly, leaving a 1/2-inch border. Cover cheese with half of the ham. Starting at one end, roll dough up very tightly, jelly-roll fashion. Repeat with remaining pastry sheet, cheese and ham. Place rolls on baking sheet and freeze until firm, at least 45 minutes.

Can be made in advance up to this point.

Preheat oven to 400°. Lightly oil 2 baking sheets.

Cut dough into 1/2-inch-thick slices. Arrange on prepared baking sheets. Brush with the egg whites. Bake until cheese is bubbly, 10 to 12 minutes. Turn baking sheets back to front and continue baking until spirals are light brown, 8 to 10 minutes. Transfer to a serving platter.

36 servings

pinach Balls

two 10-ounce packages frozen
  chopped spinach, thawed,
  drained and squeezed dry
2 cups herb stuffing mix
3 eggs, lightly beaten
4 scallions, finely chopped

1 cup firmly packed grated
  Parmesan cheese
dash nutmeg
8 tablespoons (1 stick) unsalted
  butter, melted

Preheat oven to 350°.

In a food processor grind the stuffing to make fine crumbs. Transfer to a bowl and combine together all the ingredients until thoroughly mixed. Cover and refrigerate for 2 hours.

Roll spinach mixture into walnut-size balls and arrange on ungreased baking sheets. Bake until golden, about 10 to 15 minutes. Serve hot with Mustard Sauce.

Can be made in advance. Can also be frozen and baked without thawing. Adjust baking time.

Mustard Sauce
1 egg, lightly beaten
1 cup heavy cream
a 2-ounce can dry mustard
1 1/2 tablespoons cornstarch

pinch of salt
1 cup sugar
1/2 teaspoon white vinegar

In a small bowl beat together the egg and cream until well combined. In a small saucepan mix the mustard, cornstarch, salt and sugar. Stir in the egg mixture.

Bring to a boil over low heat, whisking constantly. Remove from heat as soon as boiling point is reached. Add the vinegar and set saucepan in ice water to speed the cooling process, whisking constantly.

When mixture is cool transfer to a bowl, cover and refrigerate.

A PICNIC BEFORE THE LEVITT

FRESH FRUIT

The banks of the Saugatuck River are scenic and rich in history. Once a major shipping lane, the Saugatuck now is the site of private homes, pleasure boats and some of Westport's remaining historical buildings. Yet the river's most significant site to the Westport Young Woman's League is perhaps the Levitt Pavilion—the outdoor entertainment center it helped to build and which it continues to support through its yearly sponsorship of the Wednesday Night Children's Series. The Levitt Pavilion offers the town a summer full of free musical and theatrical events.

Chili Con Queso

1 tablespoon vegetable oil
1 large onion, chopped
1 clove garlic, minced
1 tablespoon flour
1 tablespoon chili powder
a 14-ounce can tomatoes with
  juice, chopped

a 4-ounce can diced green chilies
1/2 pound Monterey Jack cheese,
  thinly sliced
1/2 pound Cheddar cheese,
  grated
2 fresh jalapeño peppers,
  chopped

Remove seeds from jalapeño peppers with rubber gloves.

In a saucepan heat the oil and sauté the onion and garlic until soft. Add the flour and chili powder, stirring constantly. Add the tomatoes and green chilies and cook about 5 more minutes.

Lower heat and stir in the cheeses until they melt. Add the jalapeño peppers and cook 5 minutes longer.

Serve warm with tortilla chips.

Can be frozen and reheated.

Artichoke Squares

two 6-ounce jars marinated
  artichoke hearts, split lengthwise
1 small onion, minced
1 clove garlic, minced
4 eggs, beaten
1/4 cup fine dry bread crumbs
1/4 teaspoon salt

1/8 teaspoon pepper
1/8 teaspoon dried oregano
1/8 teaspoon Tabasco sauce
1/2 pound sharp Cheddar cheese,
  grated
2 tablespoons minced fresh
  parsley

Preheat oven to 325°. Butter a 7x11-inch pan.

Drain marinade from one jar of artichokes into a saucepan and sauté the onions and garlic until soft. Remove with a slotted spoon and transfer to a bowl. Discard liquid from other jar.

Mix eggs, bread crumbs and seasonings into the onion mixture. Stir in the Cheddar cheese, parsley and artichokes.

Pour into prepared pan and bake until set, about 30 minutes. Make sure center is done. Cool and cut into 1 inch squares.

Serve warm or at room temperature.   (24)

Can be made in advance and reheated.

36

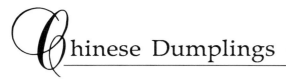hinese Dumplings

24 3 1/2-inch won ton wrappers

lettuce for lining the steamer

Filling no. 1

1/2 pound ground pork
2 tablespoons minced fresh ginger
4 scallions, finely chopped
1 tablespoon soy sauce

2 cups finely chopped Chinese
   cabbage
1 tablespoon sherry
dash of sesame oil
pepper to taste

Filling no. 2

1/2 pound ground beef
1 teaspoon minced fresh ginger
1 tablespoon soy sauce
1 tablespoon dry sherry
5 water chestnuts, minced
2 scallions, minced

2 dried Chinese mushrooms,
   soaked in warm water for 30
   minutes, discard any tough
   stems and chop finely
1/2 teaspoon sugar

Select the filling and in a bowl combine together all the ingredients. Line a bamboo steamer with lettuce leaves.

To assemble:

Place 1 heaping teaspoon of filling on each won ton wrapper. Moisten edges with water and fold dough over to form a triangle. Press with fingers to seal. Press folded edge down against a flat surface. Bend the two bottom corners of the triangle, curving them slightly. Place in the steamer. Do not let dumplings touch each other. Steam for 10 to 15 minutes, depending on filling.
Serve with Soy Ginger Sauce.

Soy Ginger Sauce

1 teaspoon minced fresh ginger
3 tablespoons soy sauce
1 tablespoon Chinese red vinegar

1/2 teaspoon sesame oil
dash of hot oil
1 scallion, minced

In a bowl combine all the ingredients and mix thoroughly.

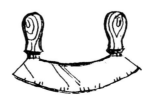

Crudités Accompaniments

Honey Sesame Dip

2 tablespoons plus 2 teaspoons
  sesame seeds, toasted
1 cup crème fraîche
1/4 cup honey

1/2 teaspoon lemon juice
tangerine slices, melon wedges,
  kiwis, other seasonal fruit

Place sesame seeds between two sheets of wax paper and crush lightly with a rolling pin. Transfer to a bowl and stir in the crème fraîche, honey and lemon juice. Mix well, cover and refrigerate until chilled.

Vegetable Dip

1 cup mayonnaise
1/2 teaspoon lemon juice
1/2 cup chopped fresh parsley
1 tablespoon grated onion
2 tablespoons chopped fresh
  chives

1/4 teaspoon salt
1/4 teaspoon paprika
1/8 teaspoon curry powder
1 clove garlic, minced
salt and pepper to taste
1/2 cup heavy cream

In a bowl combine all the ingredients except the heavy cream. Whip the cream until soft peaks form. Fold into the vegetable mixture, cover and refrigerate. Serve in hollowed out red pepper with assorted vegetables.

Seafood Dip

1 tablespoon ketchup
1 tablespoon mayonnaise
1 tablespoon paprika
1/4 teaspoon red pepper flakes
1/4 teaspoon dry mustard

3/4 teaspoon curry powder
juice of 1/2 lemon
1 clove garlic
1 teaspoon salt
1/2 teaspoon pepper

In a food processor combine all the ingredients and mix thoroughly.

Add to the mayonnaise mixture:
2 tablespoons heavy cream
1 tablespoon minced fresh parsley
1 tablespoon horseradish sauce

1/4 teaspoon celery seed
2 cups mayonnaise

Mix until well combined. Transfer to a bowl, cover and refrigerate until chilled.

Curry Dip

two 8-ounce packages cream
  cheese, softened
1/2 cup chutney
1 teaspoon dry mustard

2 teaspoons curry powder
1 pineapple
assorted vegetables or fruit

In a food processor mix together all the ingredients until just blended, 2 to 3 turns only. Transfer to a bowl, cover and refrigerate.

Cut the pineapple in half lengthwise and hollow out. Reserve fruit for another use. Spoon the dip into the hollowed pineapple.

Green Peppercorn Dip

2 teaspoons green peppercorns, packed
  in water, drained
1 cup mayonnaise

1/4 cup Dijon mustard
1 clove garlic
assorted vegetables

In a food processor blend all the ingredients well. Transfer to a bowl, cover and refrigerate until chilled.

Serve in half a red or green pepper. Arrange crudités all around.

Cucumber Dip

1 cup finely diced cucumbers,
  peeled and seeded
salt
1 cup yogurt
1/2 cup heavy cream, whipped to
  soft peaks

1 tablespoon minced fresh dill
2 cloves garlic, minced
lemon juice to taste
salt and pepper to taste

In a bowl lightly salt the cucumbers. Let stand 30 minutes. Drain well. Lightly fold the yogurt into the whipped cream. Fold in the cucumbers, dill, garlic, lemon juice and salt and pepper. Refrigerate for 1/2 hour.

Hot Anchovy Dip

3/4 cup olive oil
3 tablespoons unsalted butter
2 teaspoons finely chopped garlic

8-10 anchovy fillets, finely
  chopped
1 teaspoon salt

In a saucepan melt the butter with the oil and briefly sauté the garlic. Do not let it brown. Add the anchovy fillets and cook over low heat, stirring frequently, until the anchovies dissolve. Stir in the salt.

Transfer to a fondue pot and serve with assorted vegetable crudités.

Roquefort Cheese with Cognac

1 pound Roquefort cheese, room temperature	pinch of red pepper
	1/3 cup cognac or to taste
1 cup (2 sticks) unsalted butter, softened	

In a mixer bowl blend the cheese with the butter until creamy. Add the cayenne pepper and the cognac.

Before serving add more cognac, if needed, to spread.

Serve with toast wedges or crackers.

Can be made in advance. Will keep several weeks in a covered jar in the refrigerator.

Herb Cheese

a 3-ounce package cream cheese, softened	2 tablespoons grated Parmesan cheese
4 tablespoons (1/2 stick) unsalted butter	1 tablespoon dry white wine
1/4 teaspoon garlic powder	1 tablespoon minced fresh parsley
dash of marjoram	dash of thyme

In a food processor cream together all the ingredients. Transfer to a bowl, cover and refrigerate for 4 hours.

Serve with crackers.

Spinach-Wrapped Chicken with Oriental Dip

2 1/2 pounds chicken breasts
a 13 3/4-ounce can chicken broth
1/4 cup soy sauce

1 tablespoon Worcestershire
  sauce
1 pound fresh spinach
Oriental Dip

In a saucepan combine the chicken breasts, broth, soy sauce and Worcestershire sauce. Bring to a boil, lower heat and simmer until tender, about 15 minutes.

Remove the chicken from the broth and let cool. Remove and discard skin and bones. Cut chicken into 1-inch chunks.

Wash spinach thoroughly. Remove and discard stems and place leaves in a colander. Bring 2 quarts water to a boil and pour over leaves. Allow to drain thoroughly. Set aside to cool.

To assemble:
Place chicken chunk at the stem end of a spinach leaf. Roll over once, fold leaf in on both sides, and continue rolling around chicken. Secure end of leaf with a toothpick. Refrigerate until thoroughly chilled.

Serve with Oriental Dip.

Oriental Dip
1/2 cup sour cream
1 teaspoon sesame seeds, toasted
1/4 teaspoon ground ginger

2 teaspoons soy sauce
1 teaspoon Worcestershire sauce

In a bowl combine all the ingredients until well blended. Refrigerate until ready to serve.

50 appetizers

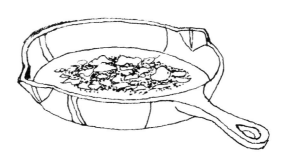

ex-Mex Layer Dip

a 10 1/2-ounce can of bean dip or
   refried beans
2 avocados
2 tablespoons lime juice
salt and pepper to taste
1 cup sour cream
1/2 cup mayonnaise
1 packet taco seasoning mix

1 bunch scallions, chopped
a 6-ounce can pitted black olives,
   chopped
2 tomatoes, chopped
1/2 pound Monterey Jack cheese,
   shredded
tortilla chips

   Spread bean dip in the bottom of a glass serving bowl. In a food
processor puree the avocados with the lime juice and salt and
pepper. Spread on top of the beans.
   In a bowl combine the sour cream, mayonnaise and seasoning
packet. Layer on top of the avocado. *Can be made in advance up
to this point.*

To assemble:
   Layer the scallions, then olives, then tomatoes, ending with the
cheese.
   Serve with tortilla chips.

Soup

$\mathcal{S}$hrimp and Cucumber Soup

2 large cucumbers, peeled, seeded
  and cut into chunks
1/4 cup red wine vinegar
1 tablespoon sugar
1 teaspoon salt
1 pound small shrimp, peeled and
  deveined

2 tablespoons unsalted butter
1/4 cup dry white vermouth
1 1/2 cups buttermilk
1/4-1/2 cup minced fresh dill
salt and white pepper to taste
dill sprigs for garnish

In a bowl toss the cucumber with the vinegar, sugar and salt. Let stand 30 minutes.

Rinse shrimp and pat dry. In a small saucepan melt the butter and cook the shrimp over high heat until pink, about 2 minutes. Remove with slotted spoon and set aside.

In the same saucepan add the vermouth and boil down until reduced to a few tablespoons. Pour over shrimp.

Drain cucumbers and transfer to a food processor. Add the buttermilk and puree the mixture. Transfer to a bowl, add the dill and shrimp and mix well. Adjust seasoning with salt and pepper. Cover and chill. Garnish with a sprig of dill.

4 to 6 servings

$\mathcal{T}$ortilla Soup

7 cups chicken broth
1 onion
2 stalks celery
1 carrot
1/2 green pepper
1/2 lemon
2 sprigs parsley
1 clove garlic
2 medium tomatoes
1 small onion
2 tablespoons vegetable oil
2 tablespoons chopped coriander

1 teaspoon chili powder
1/2 teaspoon ground cumin
1/4 cup tomato paste
salt and pepper to taste
3 corn tortillas
oil for frying
1 avocado, diced
2 cups grated Monterey Jack
  cheese
2/3 cup finely chopped onion
1 serrano chili or jalapeño
  pepper, finely chopped

In a large saucepan heat the broth and add the onion, celery, carrot, green pepper, lemon and parsley sprigs. Simmer for 15 minutes. Strain broth and discard vegetables.

In a blender mix the garlic, tomatoes and onion. Meanwhile, in a saucepan heat the oil and cook the tomato-onion mixture for about 10 minutes. Combine the onion mixture, coriander, chili powder, cumin and tomato paste with the chicken broth. Simmer for 20 minutes. Adjust seasoning with salt and pepper.

Cut tortillas in half, then into 1/2-inch strips. Deep fry in hot oil until light brown and crisp. Drain on paper towels. *Can be prepared a few days in advance.*

When ready to serve, put tortilla strips and avocado in soup bowls. Pour hot soup over them and serve immediately.

Place the cheese, onion and serrano chili in individual serving bowls and pass separately.

6 servings

Apple-Butternut Squash Soup

9 tablespoons butter
1 onion, chopped
2 leeks including 2 inches of green
   top, chopped
1/2 cup chopped celery
1/2 cup chopped carrots
1 pound butternut squash, peeled,
   seeded and chopped
1 small turnip, peeled and
   chopped
2 large tart green apples, peeled,
   cored and chopped

4 cups chicken broth
4 tablespoons flour
1 cup apple cider
1/4 teaspoon nutmeg
1/4 teaspoon dried rosemary,
   crumbled
1/4 teaspoon dried sage, crumbled
salt and pepper to taste
1/2 cup heavy cream
1/2 cup grated Gruyère cheese
croutons for garnish

In a large saucepan melt 3 tablespoons of the butter and sauté the onion, leeks and celery, stirring occasionally, until vegetables are softened. Add the carrots, squash, turnip, apples and chicken broth. Bring to a boil, lower heat and simmer until all the vegetables are softened, about 45 minutes.

In a small saucepan melt the remaining 6 tablespoons butter, add the flour and cook the roux, stirring continuously for 3 minutes. Remove the saucepan from the heat, gradually add 1 cup of the liquid from the soup mixture in a steady stream, whisking continuously to avoid lumps. Pour back into the soup mixture. Add the cider, nutmeg, rosemary, sage and salt and pepper. Simmer the soup for 10 minutes.

Before serving stir in the cream and the Gruyère cheese. Garnish with croutons.

6 to 8 servings

hestnut Soup

2 tablespoons unsalted butter
1 large onion, chopped
1 pound chestnuts, fresh or
   vacuum packed
4-5 cups chicken broth

1 stalk celery, chopped
1 carrot, chopped
1 tablespoon chopped parsley
2 tablespoons Madeira or sherry
1/4 cup heavy cream

In a large saucepan melt the butter and sauté the onions until golden. Do not allow to brown. Add the chestnuts and cook for 2 minutes.

Add the chicken broth, celery, carrot and parsley. Cover, bring to a boil, lower heat and simmer for 45 minutes. Transfer to a food processor and puree. Return to saucepan.

Before serving, add the Madeira or sherry and cream and heat through. Do not allow to boil.

6 servings

olden Squash Bisque

2 tablespoons butter
1 medium onion, chopped
1 cup chopped carrots
4 cups chopped yellow squash
1/4 teaspoon sugar
1/4 teaspoon marjoram leaves

a 13 3/4-ounce can chicken broth
1/4 cup whipping cream
ground nutmeg to taste
salt and white pepper to taste
minced parsley for garnish

In a large saucepan melt the butter and sauté the onion for 5 minutes. Add the carrots and squash and cook until onion is golden. Do not allow to brown. Add the sugar, marjoram and chicken broth. Bring to a boil, lower heat, cover and simmer for 20 minutes or until the vegetables are tender.

Puree the mixture in a food processor. Return puree to the saucepan and add the cream, nutmeg and salt and pepper. Heat thoroughly, stirring often. Garnish with the parsley.

4 to 6 servings

Oriental Vegetable Soup

1 pound boneless pork
1/4 cup dry sherry
1 tablespoon soy sauce
2 teaspoons minced fresh ginger
2 teaspoons oil
1/2 cup sliced fresh mushrooms
1/2 cup sliced bamboo shoots,
   rinsed
1/2 cup sliced water chestnuts,
   rinsed
1/2 cup sliced carrots
8 cups chicken broth
1/2 pound fresh snow peas
salt to taste
2 eggs, beaten

Slice pork across grain into thin strips 2 inches long. (Slicing will be easier if meat is partially frozen.) Combine sherry, soy sauce and ginger. Mix with the pork.

Heat oil in a wok and add the pork. Stir fry over high heat until pork is lightly browned. Stir in the mushrooms, bamboo shoots, water chestnuts, carrots and broth. Bring to a boil, lower heat and simmer 15 minutes. Add snow peas and salt. Cook 5 minutes longer.

Gradually add the eggs, stirring, until they separate into shreds. Serve immediately.

6 to 8 servings

White Gazpacho

3 medium cucumbers, peeled and
   cut into chunks
3 cups chicken broth
3 cups sour cream
3 tablespoons white vinegar
salt to taste
1 clove garlic, minced
2 tomatoes, chopped
3/4 cup chopped almonds, toasted
1/2 cup sliced scallions
1/2 cup chopped parsley

Mix cucumber chunks in a blender or food processor briefly with a little chicken broth. Transfer to a bowl and combine with the remaining broth, sour cream, vinegar, salt and garlic. Cover and chill.

Place the tomatoes, almonds, scallions and parsley in bowls and pass separately.

6 to 8 servings

47

Scallop and Mushroom Soup

6 tablespoons butter
1 large onion, finely chopped
1 carrot, chopped
2 large celery stalks, finely
   chopped
2 cups clam juice
1 cup water
2 medium potatoes, diced

a cheesecloth bag containing 1/2
   teaspoon dried thyme, 1 bay
   leaf and 3 parsley stems
1 cup heavy cream
1/2 cup white wine
3/4 pound mushrooms, sliced
1 1/2 pounds bay scallops
salt and white pepper to taste
minced fresh parsley for garnish

In a large saucepan melt 3 tablespoons of the butter and sauté the onion. Add the carrot and celery, cover and cook gently over low heat, stirring occasionally, for 3 minutes. Add the clam juice, water, potatoes and the cheesecloth bag and bring to a boil. Lower heat and simmer, covered, for 20 minutes or until the vegetables are tender. Discard the cheesecloth.

In a food processor puree the stock mixture in batches and force the puree through the fine disk of a food mill into a saucepan. Add the cream and wine and heat through.

Meanwhile, in a saucepan melt the remaining 3 tablespoons of butter and sauté the mushrooms.

Add the mushrooms and scallops to the soup. Adjust seasoning with salt and pepper. Simmer until the scallops are opaque, about 3 to 5 minutes. Garnish with the parsley.

6 servings

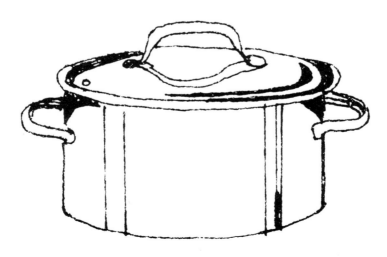

Cauliflower and Cheese Soup

2 cups chicken broth
2 carrots, sliced
1 small cauliflower, sliced
2 tablespoons butter
1 bunch scallions, including 1 inch
   of green part, chopped

5 mushrooms, sliced
2 tablespoons flour
2 cups milk
2 cups grated Cheddar cheese
3 tablespoons dry sherry
1 tablespoon chopped chives

In a large saucepan heat the chicken broth. Add the carrots and cauliflower and cook until just tender. Remove vegetables with a strainer and set aside to cool. Reserve broth.

In another saucepan melt the butter and sauté the scallions and mushrooms until soft. Sprinkle with the flour and cook 2 minutes. Gradually add the broth and cook, stirring constantly, until thickened.

Add the cauliflower and carrots to the broth. Simmer 2 minutes.

Before serving, stir in the milk and Cheddar cheese and heat until cheese melts. Stir in the sherry. Garnish with the chives.

6 servings

Avocado and Chicken Soup

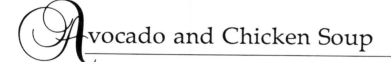

6 cups chicken broth
1 whole chicken breast
2 onions, sliced
1/2 teaspoon ground coriander

1/2 teaspoon dried oregano
salt and white pepper to taste
1 avocado, thinly sliced

In a large saucepan heat the chicken broth. Add the chicken breast, onions, coriander, oregano and salt and pepper. Bring to a boil, lower heat, cover and simmer for 20 minutes.

Remove the chicken breast and let cool. Strain the stock into another saucepan and set aside. Discard the onions.

Peel off the chicken skin and cut chicken breast into small julienne strips. Stir the strips into the broth and heat.

Before serving, add the avocado.

6 servings

Mint Yogurt Soup

2 1/2 cups beef or chicken broth
2 1/2 tablespoons unsalted butter
2 tablespoons flour
5 cups yogurt, room temperature

1/4 cup finely chopped fresh mint
  or 2 tablespoons dried mint,
  crushed
salt and white pepper to taste
sprigs of fresh mint for garnish

In a large saucepan heat the broth. Set aside.

In a small saucepan melt the butter, add the flour and blend well, stirring constantly for about 4 minutes. Do not let the flour brown. Remove from heat.

In a steady stream, add one cup of warm broth to the flour, whisking continuously. Gradually return this mixture to the remaining broth and bring back to a boil very slowly to avoid making lumps. Cook, stirring occasionally, for about 20 minutes or until the soup is thick and smooth. Remove from heat.

In a bowl stir the yogurt and gradually pour into the broth, beating vigorously. Heat the soup but do not allow it to boil or it will curdle. Stir in the mint. Adjust seasoning with salt and pepper to taste.

Garnish with a sprig of fresh mint.

May be served warm or chilled.

6 servings

Kale and Bean Soup

1 cup dried white beans
1/2 teaspoon salt
3 tablespoons olive oil
1 onion, thinly sliced
1 pound linguica or chorizo
  sausage, sliced diagonally

1 pound kale, stems removed,
  washed and coarsely chopped
a 28-ounce can of crushed Italian
  tomatoes
1 bay leaf
salt and pepper to taste

Place beans in a saucepan with water to cover, add salt and bring to a boil. Remove from heat and allow to soak overnight.

Drain the beans. In a saucepan heat the oil and sauté the onion until lightly browned. Add the beans and 5 cups water. Bring to a boil, lower heat and simmer until the beans are tender, about 2 1/2 to 3 hours.

Add the sausage, kale, tomatoes and bay leaf. Simmer until the kale is cooked, about 1 hour. Adjust seasoning with salt and pepper.

6 servings

ean Soup

1/4 cup green split peas	1/4 pound chopped ham
1/4 cup yellow split peas	1 large onion, sliced
1/4 cup kidney beans	a 14-ounce can tomatoes with
1/4 cup baby lima beans	juice, chopped
1/4 cup navy beans	2 tablespoons lemon juice
1/4 cup pinto beans	1 clove garlic, crushed
1/4 cup black-eyed peas	pinch of ginger
1/4 cup lentils	salt and pepper to taste
2 tablespoons salt	

Make the day before to allow flavors to blend.

Place the beans in a large bowl, cover with water, add salt, cover and refrigerate overnight.

Drain the beans and place in a kettle with 2 quarts of water, the ham and onion. Bring to a boil, lower heat and simmer for at least 3 hours, adding more water if necessary.

Add tomatoes, lemon juice, garlic and ginger.

Adjust seasoning with salt and pepper.

6 servings

urried Carrot Soup

3 tablespoons unsalted butter	1 cup light cream
1 medium onion, thinly sliced	1-2 teaspoons curry powder
4 cups chicken broth	1/4 teaspoon nutmeg
1 pound carrots, peeled and cut	salt to taste
into 1/2-inch slices	1 tablespoon minced chives for
1 cup orange juice	garnish

In a large saucepan melt the butter and sauté the onion until soft. Do not allow to brown.

Add the chicken broth and carrots. Bring to a boil, lower heat and simmer until carrots are tender, about 20 minutes.

Puree carrot mixture in a food processor. Return mixture to saucepan and add orange juice and cream. Stir in the curry powder, nutmeg and salt. *Can be made in advance up to this point.*

Before serving, heat the soup carefully. Do not allow to boil. Garnish with chives.

May be served hot or chilled.

6 servings

DINING BY THE POOL

In the 1930s and 1940s, Westport became home to some very special artists whose genre was that most popular of art forms—the cartoon. One of the most beloved cartoons through the years has been BLONDIE, depicting the daily trials and tribulations of the suburban Bumsteads. The creator of Dagwood, Blondie, Mr. Dithers and Daisy is Stan Drake. He and his wife Lainey have called Westport home for many years. Westporters take particular delight knowing that the Bumsteads and the Drakes are their neighbors.

Spicy Roasted Tomato Soup

Contributed by Martha Stewart, Entertaining, Westport

3 green peppers
2 1/2 quarts chicken broth
4 red peppers, sliced and sautéed
6 large onions, chopped and
   sautéed
6 large cloves garlic, chopped

2 quarts canned tomatoes, drained
   and chopped, or 6 large fresh
   tomatoes, skinned, seeded and
   coarsely chopped
2 pounds carrots, chopped
3 large parsnips
2 tablespoons curry powder
salt and pepper to taste

Broil the green peppers until the skins are black. Put the peppers in a large paper bag for 5 minutes. Remove from the bag and rub off the pepper skins. Seed and slice the peppers. Set aside.

In a saucepan bring the chicken broth to a boil and add the red peppers, onions, garlic, tomatoes, carrots, and parsnips and cook until the vegetables are tender. Add the curry powder and salt and pepper.

In a food processor puree the soup mixture. Garnish with the sliced green peppers.

6 to 8 servings

Cream of Turnip Soup

4 tablespoons (1/2 stick) unsalted
   butter
6-8 white turnips, peeled and cut
   into 1-inch chunks
3 1/2 cups chicken broth
2 cups peeled, cubed potatoes

3 cups heavy cream
1/2 teaspoon Worcestershire
   sauce
few drops Tabasco sauce
salt and white pepper to taste

In a large saucepan melt the butter and add the turnips. Cook, stirring occasionally, for about 15 minutes. Do not let turnips brown.

Add the chicken broth and potatoes and simmer until vegetables are just tender but not soft, about 20 minutes.

Puree turnip mixture in a food processor. Transfer to a bowl, cover and chill.

Before serving, stir in the cream and add the Worcestershire sauce and Tabasco sauce. Adjust seasoning with salt and pepper.

Serve chilled.

8 servings

Brunch

Oyako-Don (Eggs with Vegetables and Chicken)

Contributed by Sakura of Westport

2 large onions	1 pound boned chicken breast
2 carrots	1 tablespoon vegetable oil
1 bunch scallions	4 eggs, beaten
1 pound mushrooms	

Cut all the vegetables into long, thin slices.
Slice the chicken breast into 1/2x1-inch thin strips.
In a saucepan heat the oil and briefly sauté the chicken. Add the vegetables and stir fry until vegetables are almost cooked. Add enough Mirin Sauce to just cover the vegetable chicken mixture. Add eggs, cover and cook until done. Divide into four portions and serve over rice.

Mirin Sauce

3 cups water	2 tablespoons mirin (Japanese
2 tablespoons soy sauce	cooking wine)
	3 tablespoons sugar

In a saucepan combine all the ingredients and bring to a quick boil. Remove from heat and let stand.

4 servings

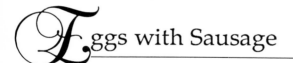# Eggs with Sausage

1 pound Italian sausage, casing removed	1/2 teaspoon salt
6 eggs, beaten	1 teaspoon dry mustard
1 1/3 cups milk	dash red pepper
5 slices white bread, cubed	3/4 cup grated cheddar cheese

Must be prepared a day in advance.

In a skillet brown the sausage. Drain well on paper towels.
In a bowl blend the eggs and milk. Add the bread cubes, salt, mustard, red pepper and the sausage.
Transfer to a 9x13-inch ovenproof baking dish. Cover and refrigerate overnight.

Preheat oven to 350°.

Sprinkle the cheddar cheese on top of the egg mixture and bake 45 minutes.

10 to 12 servings

avory Omelets

8 bacon slices
1 tablespoon vegetable oil
2 potatoes, peeled and finely
  chopped
1 leek, white part only, sliced
8 eggs

4 tablespoons (1/2 stick) unsalted
  butter
salt and white pepper
2 ounces Gruyère cheese, grated
2 tablespoons chopped fresh
  parsley

In a large skillet cook the bacon until crisp. Crumble the bacon and set aside.

Add the oil to the bacon drippings. Add the potatoes and leek and sauté until tender. Stir in the crumbled bacon.

In a large bowl beat together 2 eggs, salt and pepper. Stir in a quarter of the potato mixture and a quarter of the Gruyère cheese.

In an omelet pan melt 1 tablespoon of the butter. Pour in the egg mixture and cook over low heat until underside is browned and top is soft and moist. Sprinkle chopped parsley over top. Fold cooked omelet in half. Repeat three times with remaining ingredients.

4 servings

crambled Eggs in Croustades

12 slices of *soft* white bread,
  crusts removed
vegetable oil
8 eggs
1 tablespoon dried tarragon,
  crumbled

1/2 cup minced chives
1/4 cup milk
salt and pepper to taste
3 tablespoons unsalted butter
tarragon sprigs for garnish

Preheat oven to 350°.

Roll each slice of bread flat with a rolling pin and brush both sides of each slice with some of the oil. Fit slices gently into 12 muffin tins and bake until the edges are golden, about 20 minutes. *(Can be made a day in advance and kept in an airtight container. Reheat the croustades in a preheated 300° oven for 10 minutes.)*

In a bowl whisk together the eggs, tarragon, chives, milk and salt and pepper.

In a saucepan melt the butter and cook the egg mixture. Divide the eggs among the croustades. Garnish with the tarragon sprigs.

4 to 6 servings

Vegetable Frittata

3 tablespoons olive oil
1 onion, chopped
2 small zucchini, sliced
1 large red pepper, cut into strips
3 medium size potatoes, peeled,
 cooked, and sliced
8 pitted black olives, sliced

8 eggs, beaten
1/3 cup milk
1/2 teaspoon salt
1/4 teaspoon white pepper
1/2 cup grated Parmesan cheese
2 tablespoons chopped fresh
 parsley

Preheat oven to 350°. Line a 9-inch square baking pan with foil. Heavily butter bottom and sides.

In a large skillet heat the oil and sauté the onion for 5 minutes. Add the zucchini and red pepper and sauté until soft, about 5 minutes. Stir in the potatoes and olives. Let cool.

In a bowl combine the eggs with the milk, salt, pepper, cheese and parsley. Set aside.

Spoon vegetables into the pan, spreading them in an even layer. Pour egg mixture evenly over top. Bake until puffed and golden brown, about 35 to 40 minutes. Remove from heat and cool 10 minutes.

Use foil to lift frittata from pan. Turn down sides of foil and cut into 2-inch squares. Transfer to a serving platter.

4 to 6 servings

Baked Sausage and Eggs

1 pound sweet Italian sausage,
 casings removed
3 tablespoons unsalted butter
1/4 pound fresh mushrooms,
 sliced
1 medium red onion, chopped
12 eggs, beaten
1 cup milk

8 ounces mozzarella cheese,
 shredded
2 tomatoes, peeled and chopped
1/4 teaspoon dried oregano
salt and pepper to taste
1/3 cup grated Parmesan cheese
1/3 cup bread crumbs

Preheat oven to 400°.

In a saucepan brown the sausage, crumbling with a fork. Drain well on paper towels.

In another saucepan melt 1 tablespoon of the butter and sauté the mushrooms and onion until the onion is soft. Stir in the sausage, eggs, milk, mozzarella cheese, tomatoes, oregano and salt and pepper. Mix thoroughly.

Transfer to a shallow 3-quart ovenproof baking dish. Combine the Parmesan cheese and bread crumbs and sprinkle on top. Dot with the remaining butter. Bake until the eggs are set, about 30 to 35 minutes.

6 servings

uevos Rancheros

8 eggs	Jalapeño Sauce
1/4 cup oil for frying	sprigs of coriander for garnish
8 corn tortillas	

In a skillet heat the oil and fry the tortillas, turning them, for 30 seconds. Drain on paper towels.

Jalapeño Sauce

3 tablespoons oil	1 jalapeño pepper, seeded and
1 cup chopped onion	minced
2 green peppers, seeded and	1 teaspoon sugar
chopped	1 tablespoon minced fresh
2 cloves garlic, minced	coriander
two 35-ounce cans plum tomatoes,	salt and pepper to taste
drained and chopped	

In a saucepan heat the oil and sauté the onion, green peppers and garlic, stirring occasionally, until the onion is softened, about 5 minutes. Add the tomatoes, jalapeño pepper, sugar, coriander and salt and pepper and simmer the sauce, stirring occasionally, until thickened slightly, about 25 to 30 minutes.

Make 8 indentations in the sauce with the back of a spoon, break an egg into each indentation, and cook the eggs, covered, over moderate heat for 1 minute. Spoon a little of the sauce over the egg whites and cook the eggs, covered, spooning the sauce over the whites two or three times until they are set, about 4 minutes.

To serve:

Arrange 2 tortillas, overlapping, on a plate. Remove eggs with a slotted spoon from the Jalapeño Sauce and arrange on each tortilla. Spoon the sauce around the eggs yolks. Garnish with a sprig of coriander.

4 servings

# Blintz Soufflé

8 tablespoons (1 stick) unsalted butter, softened	1 1/2 cups sour cream
1/3 cup sugar	1/2 cup orange juice
6 eggs plus 2 egg whites	1 cup flour
	2 teaspoons baking powder

Preheat oven to 350°. Butter a 2-quart soufflé dish.

In a large bowl mix all the ingredients together until blended. Pour half the batter into the prepared dish.

Drop Blintz Filling by heaping spoonfuls over batter. With a knife, spread filling evenly. It will mix slightly with the batter. Pour remaining batter over filling. Bake until set. Serve with Blueberry Syrup.

Can be refrigerated several hours or overnight.

Blintz Filling

an 8-ounce package cream cheese, softened	2 egg yolks
1 pint small curd cottage cheese	1 tablespoon sugar
	1 teaspoon vanilla

In a bowl combine all the ingredients.

Blueberry Syrup

a 15-ounce can blueberries in syrup	dash cinnamon
1/2 cup light corn syrup	1 tablespoon cornstarch
1/2 teaspoon lemon juice	1 tablespoon cold water
dash salt	

In a small saucepan combine the blueberries, corn syrup, lemon juice, salt and cinnamon. In a small bowl, mix the cornstarch with the water and add to the blueberry mixture. Bring to a boil. Remove from heat and let cool 5 to 10 minutes.

Serve warm.

6 servings

avory Ham Roll

4 tablespoons (1/2 stick) unsalted
butter
1/2 cup flour
1/2 teaspoon salt

1/8 teaspoon white pepper
2 cups milk
5 eggs, separated
Ham Vegetable Filling

Preheat oven to 400°. Butter a 10x15-inch jelly-roll pan, line with wax paper and butter again. Dust lightly with flour.

In a saucepan melt the butter and blend in the flour, salt and pepper. Gradually stir in the milk. Bring to a boil, stirring constantly. Cook one minute. Set aside.

In a bowl beat the egg yolks and add a little hot sauce, beating continuously. Return to the saucepan and cook while continuing to beat over medium heat one minute longer. Do not boil. Cool to room temperature, stirring occasionally.

In a bowl beat the egg whites until stiff but not dry. Fold in the cooled sauce and spread in prepared pan. Bake 25 to 30 minutes.

Turn immediately onto clean kitchen towel. Spread with the warm Ham Vegetable Filling and roll with the aid of the towel. Transfer to a platter seam side down.

Ham Vegetable Filling
2 tablespoons butter
4 shallots, chopped
4 medium mushrooms, chopped
1 cup cooked chopped spinach
1 cup cooked chopped ham

1 tablespoon Dijon mustard
1/4 teaspoon nutmeg
two 3-ounce packages cream
cheese, softened
salt and pepper to taste

In a saucepan melt the butter and sauté the shallots until tender. Add the mushrooms and cook about 3 minutes. Add the spinach, ham, mustard and nutmeg. Heat thoroughly, stirring continuously. Stir in the cream cheese. Adjust seasoning with salt and pepper.

Can be made a day in advance and reheated.

6 servings

Spinach in Puff Pastry

two 10-ounce packages fresh
  spinach
4 eggs, lightly beaten
3 tablespoons farina
6 ounces feta cheese, crumbled
6 scallions, finely chopped
2/3 cup finely chopped fresh
  parsley

1/2 cup finely chopped fresh dill,
  about 1 bunch
1 teaspoon salt
pepper to taste
2 packages frozen puff pastry
  sheets, thawed *= 2 sheets* *
1 egg combined with 1 tablespoon
  water for glaze *keep cold*
                  until rolled

cover Rinse the spinach, cut off the root ends and place in a saucepan with only the water clinging to the leaves. Cook briefly until the spinach wilts. Drain and let cool in a colander. Set aside.

In a bowl combine the 4 eggs and farina (to prevent soggy pastry). Stir in the feta cheese, scallions, parsley, dill and salt and pepper. Squeeze the spinach dry, chop coarsely and combine with the cheese mixture.

Preheat oven to 350°.

To assemble:

each sheet

On a lightly floured board, roll each pastry sheet to a 12x12-inch square. Cut 9 squares. Place a rounded tablespoonful of the spinach mixture on each square. Fold in half to form a triangle and crimp with a fork. *grease sheet*

Brush top with the egg glaze. Prick top in several places with a fork. Transfer to a baking sheet. Bake for 15 minutes. *20?*

Can be prepared in advance. Freeze the triangles and bake frozen, in a 350° oven for 20 minutes.

18 pieces

Tomato and Cheese Quiche

pastry for a 10-inch quiche pan
2 tablespoons unsalted butter
1 large leek (white part only),
   thinly sliced
3 eggs, beaten
1 cup heavy cream
1/2 teaspoon sugar
3 tablespoons minced fresh
   parsley

1/2 teaspoon dried thyme
1 teaspoon dried basil
salt and pepper to taste
a 28-ounce can whole tomatoes,
   drained and coarsely chopped
3/4 pound Cheddar cheese,
   coarsely grated

Preheat oven to 400°.

Prepare pastry shell. With a fork prick the bottom of the pastry shell and line with wax paper. Fill the shell with dried beans and bake 10 minutes. Remove paper and beans. Cool slightly.

In a saucepan melt the butter and sauté the leek until tender. Set aside.

In a bowl combine the eggs with the cream, sugar, parsley, thyme, basil and salt and pepper.

In another bowl mix together the leek, tomatoes, cheese and egg mixture. Pour into quiche pan.

Bake for 15 minutes. Reduce oven to 350° and bake until center is set, about 30 minutes longer.

Let stand 10 minutes before serving.

8 servings

Green Chili Rellenos

Rellenos

1 pound sharp Cheddar cheese, grated
two 4-ounce cans whole green chilies

1 package egg roll skins
milk
oil for frying
Green Chili Sauce

Place about 1/4 cup Cheddar cheese and half a green chili in the center of each egg roll skin. Fold up, envelope style. Brush edges with milk and press to seal.

In a deep skillet heat the oil and place relleno envelope seam side up and fry until crisp. Turn and fry until other side is crisp. Drain on paper towels. Serve with Green Chili Sauce on top.

8 to 10 rellenos

Green Chili Sauce

1 tablespoon olive oil
1 onion, chopped
2 cloves garlic, crushed
1 pound cooked pork, cubed
a 14-ounce can whole tomatoes, drained and chopped

two 4-ounce cans chopped green chilies
1 teaspoon ground cumin
dash Tabasco sauce

In a saucepan heat the oil and sauté the onion and garlic. Add the pork and stir 1 minute. Add the tomatoes, green chilies, cumin and Tabasco sauce. Bring to a boil, lower heat and simmer 1 hour. *Can be made in advance.*

4 servings

Asparagus Spears

16 asparagus spears, trimmed
1/2 cup soft herb garlic cheese, room temperature

10 slices prosciutto ham, approximately

Steam asparagus until crisp tender. Rinse in cold water. Cut prosciutto ham in half unless slices are small.

Spread cheese on prosciutto ham. Wrap around asparagus spears.

$\mathcal{L}$eek and Mushroom Quiche

1 unbaked 9-inch deep dish
   pastry shell
2 tablespoons unsalted butter
1/2 cup chopped onions
1/2 cup chopped leeks, white
   part only

1/2 cup sliced mushrooms
pinch of nutmeg
salt and pepper to taste
6 ounces grated Gruyère cheese
1 cup heavy cream
2 eggs, well beaten

Preheat oven to 425°.

With a fork prick the bottom of the pastry shell and line with wax paper. Fill the shell with dried beans and bake 10 minutes. Do not let it brown. Remove paper and beans. Cool slightly.
   Reduce oven heat to 350°.
   In a saucepan melt the butter and sauté the onions until soft. Add the leeks and mushrooms and cook until heated thoroughly. Add the nutmeg and salt and pepper to taste.
   Pour onion and mushroom mixture into partially baked crust. Sprinkle the top with the Gruyère cheese.
   In a saucepan scald the heavy cream and slowly add the eggs being careful that they don't curdle. Pour over cheese and bake until custard is set, about 25 to 30 minutes. Let cool 10 minutes before serving.

To freeze:
   Bake the shell and cool. Freeze for about 45 minutes. Prepare the quiche but do not bake. Freeze, uncovered. When frozen, cover with foil until ready to use.
   Bake in a 450° oven for 15 minutes. Lower oven heat to 350° and bake for 50 minutes longer or until center is set.

6 servings

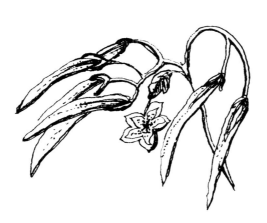

Crêpes with Chicken Mushroom Filling

Crêpe Batter

2/3 cup flour
2 eggs
1/8 teaspoon salt

3 tablespoons butter, melted
1 cup milk

Must be prepared in advance.
In a mixer bowl beat the flour, eggs, salt, butter and 1/2 cup of the milk until smooth. Add remaining milk and blend well. Cover and let batter rest for 1 hour or refrigerate overnight.

Heat skillet or crêpe pan and brush lightly with melted butter. Ladle a scant 1/4 cup of batter into the middle of the pan. Quickly tilt pan to cover entire bottom with a thin layer. Cook about 1 minute. Turn the crêpe over with a spatula and cook until lightly browned, about 30 seconds. Repeat with remaining batter.

Crêpes can be made in advance. Wrap them in plastic wrap and refrigerate or freeze until ready to use.

Chicken Mushroom Filling

1/4 cup butter
3/4 pound mushrooms, sliced
1/2 cup chopped scallions

2 1/2 cups diced cooked chicken
1/2 cup sherry
salt and pepper to taste

In a skillet melt the butter. Add the mushrooms and scallions and sauté until scallions are soft. Add the sherry and cook over high heat until all the liquids have evaporated. Adjust seasoning with salt and pepper.

Cream Sauce

1/4 cup flour
2/3 cup sherry
1 cup chicken broth
2 cups light cream

1/2 teaspoon salt
1/4 teaspoon pepper
1/2 cup grated Swiss cheese

In a saucepan combine the flour, sherry, broth, cream, salt and pepper. Heat through over low heat. Reserve Swiss cheese for topping.

Combine filling with half of the Cream Sauce.

To assemble:

Preheat oven to 425°.
Place 3 to 4 tablespoons of the chicken mixture on each crêpe and roll up. Place the crêpes in a baking dish large enough to

hold them in one layer and top with remaining sauce. Sprinkle with the reserved Swiss cheese. *Crêpes can be refrigerated or frozen at this point.*

Bake for 15 minutes.

8 to 12 crêpes

Apple and Cinnamon Pancakes

3 cups flour
1/2 cup sugar
4 teaspoons baking powder
1 teaspoon salt
1/2 teaspoon ground allspice
1 teaspoon cinnamon
2 1/2 cups milk, room temperature
4 eggs

6 tablespoons (3/4 stick) unsalted
  butter, melted
1/2 teaspoon vanilla
4 tablespoons (1/2 stick) butter
6 large tart green apples, peeled,
  cored and cut into thin slices
6 tablespoons sugar
1 1/2 teaspoons cinnamon
Cinnamon Sugar

Must be prepared in advance.

In a large bowl mix the flour, sugar, baking powder, salt, allspice and cinnamon. In another bowl, lightly beat together the 2 cups milk, eggs, melted butter and vanilla. Add to dry ingredients and mix until just blended. Cover and refrigerate 1 to 2 hours.

In a saucepan melt the 4 tablespoons butter. Add the apples, sugar and cinnamon and cook until apples begin to soften, stirring occasionally, 3 to 5 minutes. Transfer to a bowl and let cool.

Stir the pancake batter. Thin to a pouring consistency with remaining 1/2 cup milk, if necessary.

In a large skillet melt 1/2 teaspoon butter. Ladle about 1/2 cup of batter onto skillet. Top with 2 tablespoons apple mixture. Cook until bubbles begin to appear on surface of pancakes, about 3 minutes. Turn and cook until bottoms are golden brown and pancakes are cooked through, 2 to 3 minutes. Transfer to a heated platter and top with remaining apple mixture. Sprinkle with the Cinnamon *Sugar*. Serve with maple syrup.

8 pancakes

Cinnamon Sugar
1/4 cup sugar   1/2 teaspoon cinnamon

Combine the sugar and cinnamon.

Crêpes with Ham Spinach Filling

Crêpe Batter

2 large eggs
1 cup flour
1 tablespoon vegetable oil

1/8 teaspoon salt
1 1/3 cups milk

Must be prepared in advance.

In a mixer bowl combine the eggs, flour, oil and salt and beat until smooth. Gradually add the milk, beating continuously. Let batter rest at least 2 hours or refrigerate overnight.

Heat skillet or crêpe pan and brush lightly with melted butter. Ladle a scant 1/4 cup of batter into the middle of the pan. Quickly tilt pan to cover entire bottom with a thin layer. Cook about 1 minute. Turn the crêpe over with a spatula and cook until lightly browned, about 30 seconds. Repeat with remaining batter.

Crêpes can be made in advance. Wrap them in plastic wrap and refrigerate or freeze until ready to use.

16 crêpes

Ham Spinach Filling

1 1/2 pounds fresh spinach
1/3 cup grated Parmesan cheese
1/4 cup chopped fresh parsley
1 clove garlic
4 scallions, coarsely chopped
2 eggs

1 cup ricotta cheese
1 cup cooked ham or chicken,
    coarsely chopped
1/8 teaspoon nutmeg
salt and pepper to taste

Rinse spinach and with only the water remaining on the leaves, cook, stirring occasionally, until spinach is wilted. Run under cold water. Pat dry on paper towels.

In a food processor combine the Parmesan cheese, parsley, garlic and scallions. Add the spinach and eggs and puree the mixture. Add the ricotta cheese and mix well. Transfer to a bowl, stir in the ham and nutmeg. Adjust seasoning with salt and pepper.

Tomato Sauce

4 tomatoes, peeled, seeded and
    finely chopped

1/3 cups grated Parmesan cheese
1 tablespoon minced fresh basil

Combine the tomatoes with the Parmesan cheese and basil. Set aside.

Mornay Sauce

6 tablespoons unsalted butter
6 tablespoons flour
3 cups milk
1/2 cup shredded mozzarella
  cheese

1/2 cup grated Parmesan cheese
dash of nutmeg
salt and white pepper to taste

In a saucepan melt the butter and add the flour. Cook over low heat, stirring continuously with a whisk, for 3 minutes. Do not allow to brown. Pour the milk in a steady stream, while continuing to stir, until thickened. Remove from heat and allow to cool slightly.

Gently stir in the cheeses. Add nutmeg and adjust seasoning with salt and pepper.

Preheat oven to 375°. Butter a 10x14-inch ovenproof baking dish.

To assemble:

Spread Tomato Sauce in bottom of the baking dish. Divide Ham Spinach Filling among 16 crepes and roll each one up. Place rolled crêpes, seam side down, in one layer in the baking dish. *Crêpes can be frozen at this point. Defrost completely before baking.* Pour the Mornay Sauce on top.

Bake until browned, about 35 to 40 minutes.

8 servings

opover Pancake

1/2 cup flour
1/2 cup milk
2 eggs, lightly beaten
pinch of nutmeg

4 tablespoons (1/2 stick) unsalted
  butter
2 tablespoons confectioners' sugar
juice of 1/2 lemon (optional)
marmalade (optional)

Preheat oven to 425°.

Combine the flour, milk, eggs and nutmeg. Beat lightly, leaving batter a little lumpy.

Meanwhile, melt the butter in a 10-inch ovenproof skillet until hot but not burning. Pour in the batter. Bake 15 to 20 minutes until popover is puffed and golden brown. Sprinkle with the sugar and return briefly to the oven. Remove and sprinkle with lemon juice or top with marmalade, if desired.

Cut into serving pieces and serve immediately.

4 servings

BREAKFAST IN BED

ORANGE OR GRAPEFRUIT JUICE

FRESH RASPBERRIES

Breakfast in bed is definitely a luxury nowadays. Most of the League members lead active and demanding lives. Some pursue full or part-time careers, others combine busy family lives with a full schedule of volunteer activities in our community. Nevertheless, once in a while, on a lovely Sunday morning, it's a welcome change to have a special moment all to oneself.

# uffed Toast

6 slices of homemade-type white
   bread, crusts removed and the
   slices quartered diagonally
2 cups flour
4 teaspoons baking powder
1/2 cup sugar
1/2 teaspoon salt
1/2 teaspoon cinnamon
1/2 teaspoon nutmeg
1 large egg, lightly beaten
1 1/2 cups milk
2 teaspoons vegetable oil plus
   additional for frying
1 teaspoon vanilla
1/4 cup confectioners' sugar
maple syrup

Must begin a day in advance.

Let the bread dry, uncovered, overnight.

In a large bowl mix together the flour, baking powder, sugar, salt, cinnamon and nutmeg. Whisk in the egg, milk, 2 teaspoons of the oil and the vanilla until the mixture is well combined.

Dip the bread triangles into the batter, coating them completely and letting the excess drip off. Fry them in batches in 2 inches of oil for 30 seconds on each side. Transfer the puffed toasts to paper towels to drain. Sprinkle confectioners' sugar over puffed toasts. Serve with maple syrup.

6 servings

# ruit Salad

1 mango
1 papaya
4 peaches
2 kiwi
1 pint blueberries
1 medium honeydew melon
3/4 cup orange juice
3 tablespoons sugar
Vanilla Yogurt
Crème Fraîche

Must be prepared in advance.

Peel and slice the mango, papaya, peaches and kiwi. Wash and drain the blueberries. Cut melon balls from honeydew with a melon ball cutter. Mix all the fruit together.

Combine the orange juice with the sugar and pour over all. Toss fruit salad gently. Cover and refrigerate for one to two hours.

Serve with Vanilla Yogurt or Crème Fraîche.

8 to 10 servings

rapefruit Sorbet

1 tablespoon unflavored gelatin	5 cups grapefruit juice, freshly
1/4 cup cold water	squeezed
2 cups sugar	6-8 oranges
1 cup hot water	fresh mint for garnish

In a small bowl soften the gelatin in the 1/4 cup cold water. Set aside.

In a saucepan combine the sugar and hot water. Boil for 2 minutes. Remove from heat. Add the softened gelatin to the hot mixture. Add the grapefruit juice. Let cool completely.

Freeze in an ice cream maker according to manufacturer's directions.

1 1/2 quarts

To serve:

Cut a slice from the top of each orange. Hollow out and reserve pulp for another use.

Place a scoop of sorbet into each hollowed orange. Cover with sliced top. Decorate with a sprig of fresh mint.

6 to 8 servings

ruit Curry

3 tablespoons unsalted butter	1/4 cup raw cashews, halved
1 tablespoon curry powder	1/4 cup Brazil nuts, coarsely
1/2 teaspoon ground ginger	chopped
2 bananas, sliced	1/4 cup almonds, toasted
2 apples, sliced	1/2 cup raisins
2 pears, sliced	1 tablespoon honey
2 peaches, sliced	1 cup fresh orange juice
1/4 pound seedless grapes	

In a large saucepan melt the butter and stir in the curry powder and ginger. Add the fruit one kind at a time, tossing gently each time to coat with the butter. Add the nuts and raisins. Continue tossing until the fruit juices begin to bubble. Add the honey and orange juice. Lower heat, cover and simmer for 20 to 30 minutes, stirring occasionally, to prevent sticking.

4 to 6 servings

Cinnamon Butterfly Rolls

1/2 cup sugar
1 package dry yeast
4 1/3 cups flour
1 cup milk
8 tablespoons (1 stick) unsalted
 butter
1 teaspoon salt
2 teaspoons vanilla

1 egg
1/2 cup brown sugar
1/2 cup chopped pecans
1/2 cup raisins
1 teaspoon cinnamon
4 tablespoons (1/2 stick) unsalted
 butter, melted
1 egg, beaten

In a bowl mix the sugar, yeast and 1 cup flour.

In a saucepan heat the milk and the 8 tablespoons butter until warm. With mixer at low speed, beat liquid into dry ingredients. Add the salt. Increase to medium speed and beat 2 minutes. Beat in the vanilla, egg, 1 cup flour and beat 2 minutes longer. Stir in 2 cups flour. Knead dough 10 minutes, working in about 1/3 cup remaining flour. Place in oiled bowl, turning to coat top.

Cover and let rise in warm place until doubled, about 1 1/2 hours. Punch dough down. Turn onto floured surface. Cover for 15 minutes.

Oil two baking sheets.

In a bowl mix the brown sugar, pecans, raisins and cinnamon.

Cut dough in half and roll each in a 17x12-inch rectangle. Brush each with the melted butter, top with half of the sugar mixture. Roll dough tightly, jelly-roll fashion, starting with the 17-inch side. Cut into 9 wedges, 2 1/2 inches at wide side, 1 inch at short side.

Turn wedges short side up. Press handle of wooden spoon across each to form butterfly shape. Place on baking sheets and let rise until doubled.

Preheat oven to 350°.

Brush rolls with remaining egg. Bake until golden, about 20 minutes.

18 rolls

Pecan Sticky Buns

Prepare the dough as above but use a 9x13-inch baking pan. Oil the sides of the pan. Omit the pecans from the brown sugar and set them aside.

After rolling the dough, cut it into 1-inch slices. In a bowl prepare a mixture of 1/3 cup melted butter with 1/2 cup brown sugar, 2 tablespoons light corn syrup and 1 teaspoon cinnamon. Spread the sugar mixture on the bottom of prepared pan. Sprinkle the pecans on top. Place the rolls on top of the pecans, cover pan and let rise until doubled.

Bake until golden, about 20 to 30 minutes. Let the buns cool in the pan for only 5 minutes.   Invert pan onto serving platter and scrape remaining caramel onto the rolls.

reakfast Muffins

1/3 cup unsalted butter	1 1/2 teaspoons baking powder
1/2 cup sugar	1/2 teaspoon salt
1 egg	1/4 teaspoon nutmeg
1 1/2 cups flour	1/2 cup milk

Preheat oven to 350°. Butter 12 muffin tins.

In a bowl blend together the flour, baking powder, salt and nutmeg. Set aside.

In a food processor mix thoroughly the butter, sugar and egg. Add the dry ingredients to the butter mixture alternating with the milk and ending with milk. Fill muffin tins 2/3 full.

Bake until golden brown, about 20 to 25 minutes.

8 tablespoons (1 stick) unsalted	1/2 cup sugar
butter, melted	1 teaspoon cinnamon

Roll hot muffins in melted butter, then in combined sugar and cinnamon.

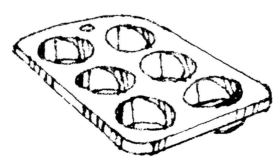

cones

1/2 cup currants	1/3 cup unsalted butter
2 1/2 cups flour, sifted	1 egg, beaten
1/2 cup sugar	1 tablespoon water
2 teaspoons baking powder	1 cup sour cream
1 teaspoon baking soda	grated rind of 1/2 lemon

Preheat oven to 425°. Butter a baking sheet.

In a small bowl toss the currants in 2 tablespoons of the flour.

In a large bowl resift the remaining flour with the sugar, baking powder and baking soda. Cut in the butter until the mixture resembles coarse meal.

In another bowl mix the egg with the water and add to the flour mixture. Stir in the sour cream, currants and lemon rind and mix well.

Divide dough into 24 balls. Flatten to 1/2-inch thick round cakes and place on the baking sheet. Bake until golden brown, about 12 minutes.

offee Cake

2 cups flour	2 eggs
1 teaspoon baking powder	1 cup sour cream
1 teaspoon baking soda	1 teaspoon vanilla
8 tablespoons (1 stick) unsalted butter	1/4 cup sugar
	2 teaspoons cinnamon
1 cup sugar	1/4 cup chopped walnuts

Preheat oven to 350°. Butter and flour a 9-inch round pan.

In a bowl combine the flour, baking powder and baking soda.

In a mixer bowl beat the butter, sugar and eggs until creamy. Add the sour cream and vanilla.   Stir in the flour mixture.

Mix together the sugar, cinnamon and walnuts.

Pour half of the batter into the prepared pan. Sprinkle half of the walnut mixture over the batter. Pour in the rest of the batter and cover with the remaining walnut mixture.

Bake for 35 to 40 minutes.

10 servings

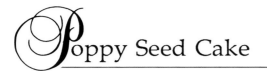oppy Seed Cake

1/2 cup poppy seeds	1/2 cup unsalted butter, softened
3/4 cup milk	1 2/3 cups sugar
2 cups flour	4 eggs
1/2 teaspoon salt	1 teaspoon vanilla
2 1/2 teaspoons baking powder	confectioners' sugar

Bake the day before to allow the flavors to mellow.
In a small saucepan combine the poppy seeds and milk and heat until milk is just warm. Set aside.

Preheat oven to 325°. Butter and flour a 10-inch bundt pan.

In a bowl mix together the flour, salt and baking powder. Set aside.
In a mixer bowl cream the butter and sugar. Beat in the eggs, one at a time. Add the vanilla.
With a wooden spoon gently stir the dry ingredients into the creamed mixture alternating with the poppy seed-milk mixture.
Pour batter into prepared pan. Bake until the cake just begins to leave sides and a cake tester inserted in the center comes out clean, about 50 to 60 minutes.
Let cake cool in pan for at least 20 minutes. Invert onto cake plate.
Before serving, sift confectioners' sugar over the top.

8 to 10 servings

$\mathcal{B}$lueberry Flummery

1 quart fresh blueberries or
   strawberries, reserving a few for
   the top
1 cup sugar
2 tablespoons water
dash of cinnamon

10-12 slices day-old homemade-
   type bread, crusts trimmed
8 tablespoons (1 stick) unsalted
   butter, melted
1 cup heavy cream
confectioners' sugar

Must be prepared a day in advance.

In a saucepan combine 3/4 cup of the blueberries, sugar and the water. Bring to a boil, lower heat and simmer 4 to 5 minutes, stirring frequently. Combine with the remaining blueberries and cinnamon. Remove from heat.

Brush both sides of the bread slices with the butter. Line the bottom of an 8-inch square pan with the bread.

Spoon some of the blueberries over the bread and top with more bread. Continue layering, ending with the bread. Cover with plastic wrap. Weight top with a heavy weight and chill overnight.

Before serving, whip cream and sweeten to taste. Spread on top and decorate with the reserved blueberries. Cut into squares.

each Clafouti

5 ripe peaches, peeled and sliced
1/2 cup blanched almonds
1/2 cup sugar
1 1/2 cups milk
2/3 cup flour

1/4 teaspoon almond extract
1/8 teaspoon salt
3 eggs
1/2 cup heavy cream
2 tablespoons confectioners' sugar

Preheat oven to 350°. Butter a 10-inch glass pie pan.

Reserve a few peach slices for decoration. Place remaining slices in glass pie pan.

In a food processor blend the almonds and sugar until almonds are finely ground. Add the milk, the flour, almond extract, salt and eggs and blend until smooth, about 30 seconds. Pour batter evenly over fruit.

Bake until top is golden and toothpick inserted in center comes out clean, about 45 to 50 minutes.

In a small bowl beat the heavy cream and sugar until soft peaks form. Spoon whipped cream onto the warm clafouti. Decorate with the reserved peach slices.

Can also be made with blueberries, strawberries or other seasonal fruit.

Apple Dumplings

1/2 cup sugar
1/4 cup light brown sugar
1/4 teaspoon nutmeg
1/2 teaspoon cinnamon
1/2 package frozen puff pastry
(1 sheet), thawed

3 tart green apples, peeled, cored
and halved
4 teaspoons unsalted butter
Apple Syrup

Preheat oven to 400°.

In a small bowl mix the sugars, nutmeg and cinnamon. Set aside.

On a lightly floured surface, roll out the puff pastry sheet to a 8x12-inch rectangle. Divide into 6 squares.

Roll each apple in the sugar mixture to coat and place in the center of the square. Fill apple core with 1 teaspoon each of butter and sugar mixture. Reserve the remaining sugar mixture. Moisten edges of pastry with water. Bring opposite corners of pastry together over apples. Pinch seams and corners to seal. *Can be made in advance up to this point.*

Place wrapped apples on ungreased baking sheet. Bake until pastry is puffed and golden brown, about 20 to 30 minutes.

Serve warm, plain or with Apple Syrup.

Apple Syrup
2 tart green apples, peeled, cored
and sliced thinly
the reserved sugar mixture

1/2 cup water
1/2 teaspoon vanilla

In a small saucepan combine all the ingredients and cook, stirring occasionally, until the apples are very soft, about 20 minutes.

Salad

sparagus with Raspberry Vinaigrette

2 pounds cooked asparagus, trimmed

1 1/2 cups raspberries

Cut the asparagus into thirds. Toss the asparagus and raspberries gently with the Raspberry Vinaigrette. Chill well before serving.

Raspberry Vinaigrette
1/4 cup raspberry vinegar
1 1/2 teaspoons honey or to taste

1 tablespoon walnut oil
1/2 cup peanut oil

In a bowl mix together the vinegar and honey. Slowly whisk in the oils in a steady stream.

6 servings

Strawberries may be substituted. Cut the strawberries in half before tossing with the asparagus. Use strawberry vinegar.

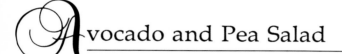vocado and Pea Salad

two 10-ounce packages frozen petit peas, thawed
4 scallions, chopped

1/4 pound mushrooms, thinly sliced
2 avocados, peeled and diced

Must be prepared in advance.

In a serving bowl combine the peas, scallions, mushrooms and avocado with enough dressing to coat salad. Mix lightly. Cover and refrigerate at least one hour.

Dressing
1 packet Hidden Valley Ranch Dressing

1 cup mayonnaise
1 cup milk

In a bowl combine the Ranch Dressing with the mayonnaise and milk.

8 servings

Marinated Bean Salad

2 cups dried beans (choose 3 kinds
   for color and appearance)
1 clove garlic, crushed
1 green pepper, coarsely chopped
2 tomatoes, coarsely chopped

1/4 cup chopped fresh parsley
6 scallions, chopped
Vinaigrette Dressing
salt and pepper to taste

Must begin a day in advance.

Pick over and rinse beans. In a saucepan cover the beans with water and bring to a boil. Remove from heat cover and let soak overnight. (If the beans are of different size, they must be soaked and cooked separately.)

Cook the beans in lightly salted water with the garlic. Simmer until tender, one hour or longer. Drain and cool.

Combine the beans with the green pepper, tomatoes, parsley and scallions. Add vinaigrette and toss well. *Allow to marinate one hour.*

Before serving, adjust seasoning with salt and pepper. Serve at room temperature.

Vinaigrette Dressing
2 tablespoons balsamic vinegar
1 tablespoon Dijon mustard
1 egg yolk
1/2 teaspoon salt

1/2 teaspoon pepper
1 teaspoon dried oregano
1/2 cup olive oil
1/4 cup vegetable oil

In a bowl whisk together the vinegar, mustard, egg yolk, salt and pepper and oregano until well mixed.

Combine the oils and gradually add to the vinegar mixture, whisking constantly until well blended.

8 servings

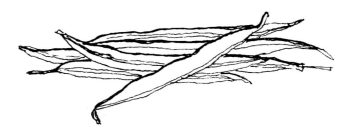

Beef and Asparagus Salad

3 tablespoons chopped shallots
1 1/2 tablespoons soy sauce
2 tablespoons olive oil
1 1/2 teaspoons thyme
juice of 1/2 lemon
pepper to taste

1 1/2 pounds flank steak
2 pounds cooked asparagus, cut
   diagonally into 2-inch pieces
1/2 bunch cooked broccoli florets,
   stems reserved for another use

Must begin a day in advance.

In a deep bowl combine the shallots, soy sauce, olive oil, thyme, lemon juice and pepper. Add the steak and marinate in the refrigerator overnight.

Reserve the marinade. Broil the steak 5 to 6 minutes on each side. Let rest 10 minutes. Cut into thin strips. Combine with the reserved marinade, asparagus, broccoli and the Ginger Soy Sauce Dressing. Toss to coat thoroughly. Cover and marinate 1 hour at room temperature.

Ginger Soy Sauce Dressing
1/3 cup soy sauce
1/4 cup white vinegar
3 tablespoons sesame oil

1 teaspoon grated fresh ginger
1 teaspoon sugar
salt and pepper to taste

Combine all the ingredients.

6 servings

eet and Red Onion Salad

5 large fresh beets with stems and leaves	salt and pepper to taste
1 large onion, thinly sliced	chopped fresh parsley
1 teaspoon dried oregano	Vinaigrette Dressing

Must be prepared in advance.

Choose beets with unblemished leaves. Cut off the stems about one inch above the beet and set them aside. Rinse beets under cold running water.

In a saucepan place the whole beets and cover with boiling water. Simmer until tender, about 45 minutes. The beets are ready when a fork pierced through the beet meets just a slight resistance. Drain and let cool.

Meanwhile, rinse the stems and leaves well in several changes of cold water. Cut the leaves from the stems and chop coarsely. Set aside. Cut the stems into 1-inch lengths.

In a saucepan place the stems, cover with boiling water and cook about 3 minutes. Add the reserved beet leaves and continue cooking until leaves are just tender, about 5 more minutes. Drain and cool.

When the beets are cool enough to handle, cut off the stem and root and remove the skin. Halve the beets lengthwise, slice thin lengthwise. Place the beets in a serving bowl and combine with the onion and beet stems and leaves. Add the Vinaigrette Dressing and mix thoroughly. Allow to marinate at least one hour.

Before serving, sprinkle the parsley over all.

Vinaigrette Dressing

2 tablespoons tarragon vinegar	1/2 cup safflower oil
1 teaspoon dried oregano	salt and pepper to taste
1/2 cup olive oil	

In a small bowl combine the vinegar and oregano. Combine the oils and add to the vinegar in a steady stream, whisking constantly until well combined. Add salt and pepper.

6 to 8 servings

roccoli Salad

2 - 3 bunches of broccoli, washed and cut into florets with a 2-inch stem, reserving the stalks for another use	1 1/2 cups olive oil
	2 tablespoons chopped fresh dill
	2 tablespoons sugar
	1 tablespoon MSG*
1 garlic head, separated and peeled	1 teaspoon salt
	1 teaspoon pepper
1/2 cup white vinegar	1 teaspoon garlic powder
1/2 cup apple cider	

Must be prepared a day in advance.

In a bowl combine all the ingredients except the broccoli. Pour marinade over broccoli. Cover and refrigerate overnight, turning occasionally.

 In this salad, the MSG is an important ingredient.

8 to 10 servings

arrot Salad

1/2 pound carrots	1/2 teaspoon dried oregano
2 cloves garlic, crushed	2 tablespoons red wine vinegar
salt and pepper to taste	olive oil

Must be prepared a day in advance.

Cook the carrots in lightly salted water until tender but firm, about 8 minutes.

Drain carrots and cut lengthwise into 2-inch strips, about 1/4-inch thick. Place in a small deep serving dish.

Bury the garlic in the carrots. Add salt and pepper, the oregano, vinegar and enough oil to cover carrots.

Cover and refrigerate overnight. Drain and remove garlic. Allow carrots to come to room temperature before serving.

4 servings

auliflower Slaw

1 head of cauliflower, trimmed
  and separated into small
  florets
1/2 head of cabbage, cored and
  finely shredded
2 stalks of celery, thinly sliced

1/2 cup sliced radishes
1/4 cup finely chopped scallions
2 tablespoons chopped fresh
  parsley
1/2 teaspoon celery seed
French Dressing

Must be prepared in advance.

In a large saucepan blanch the cauliflower in boiling salted water for 2 minutes. Drain and refresh it under running cold water.

In a serving bowl combine the cauliflower with the remaining ingredients. Add the French Dressing and toss well. Cover and marinate for one hour.

French Dressing
2 tablespoons lemon juice
salt and pepper to taste

1/2 teaspoon Dijon mustard
1/2 cup olive oil

In a bowl combine the lemon juice, salt and pepper and mustard. Add the oil in a steady stream and beat until well combined.

8 servings

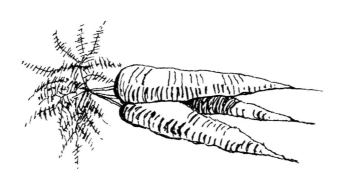

A SUNDAY NIGHT SUPPER

A FALL DINNER

There's no doubt that cooking and eating are favored League activities. When summer ends and our beautiful New England autumn begins, countless volunteer hours are spent baking breads and cookies for our Boutique Sales at the Creative Arts Festival. Those who prefer not to cook often find themselves filling the bean jars seen on top of the stove, the main ingredients for a favorite League recipe for Bean soup, a long-time best seller at the Creative Arts Festival.

One very special and personal League get-together is the Daytime Ladies Gourmet group. The third Tuesday of each month, an enthusiastic group can be found preparing a multi-course luncheon just for the pleasure of eating good food and enjoying pleasant company. Members who participate in these luncheons can either hostess or cook and many hours go into planning elaborate menus. It's a wonderful opportunity for members to share their kitchens and to pass on a favorite recipe or a culinary discovery.

Chicken Salad with Jícama

2 cups cooked chicken breasts, cut into 1/2-inch pieces
1 cup mayonnaise
2 tablespoons chopped fresh coriander
2 teaspoons chopped fresh parsley
2 teaspoons chopped fresh chives
2 tablespoons diced red pepper
2 tablespoons diced yellow pepper
2 tablespoons diced carrot
1/4 cup red seedless grapes, cut into slivers
1/4 cup julienned jicama
1/3 cup snow peas, blanched
1/4 cup slivered almonds, toasted
salt and pepper to taste

In a bowl mix the mayonnaise with the coriander, parsley and chives. Set aside.

In a large mixing bowl combine the chicken with the remaining ingredients. Add the seasoned mayonnaise and combine well. Adjust seasoning with salt and pepper.

4 servings

Curried Chicken Salad

5 cups cooked chicken, cut into bite-size pieces
an 8–ounce can water chestnuts, drained, rinsed and sliced
1 1/2 pounds seedless grapes, halved
2 cups chopped celery
2 1/2 cups sliced almonds, toasted
2 1/2 cups mayonnaise
1 tablespoon curry powder or to taste
2 tablespoons soy sauce
2 tablespoons lemon juice

Must be prepared in advance.

In a bowl combine the chicken, water chestnuts, grapes, celery and 1 1/2 cups of the almonds.

In another bowl mix the mayonnaise, curry powder, soy sauce and lemon juice. Pour over the chicken and toss to mix well. Cover and chill several hours.

Before serving, top with the remaining almonds.

4 to 6 servings

Chicken and Artichoke Salad

2 pounds cooked chicken breasts, boned and cut into bite-size pieces

an 8-ounce package chicken rice-vermicelli mix

two 6-ounce jars marinated artichoke hearts, quartered, reserving liquid

3/4 cup mayonnaise

1/2 teaspoon curry powder or to taste

4 scallions, chopped

10 pimiento-stuffed green olives, sliced (optional)

1 green pepper, chopped

Must be prepared in advance.

Cook rice (steam, not fried method), according to package directions, omitting the butter.

In a bowl mix the oil from one jar of the marinated artichokes with the mayonnaise and curry. Add the scallions, olives, green pepper and chicken. Toss well. Combine with the rice, cover and chill for several hours.

+ artich. hearts

6 servings

Corn and Red Pepper Salad

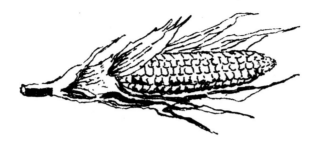

4 ears corn, husks and silk
  removed
1 red pepper, cut into thin strips
2 stalks celery, thinly sliced

2 scallions, thinly sliced
1 tablespoon chopped fresh
  coriander

Must be prepared in advance.

Cook the corn until crisp tender, about 3 minutes. Drain and cool. Cut the kernels from the cobs. Transfer the corn to a large bowl and add the red pepper, celery and scallions. Sprinkle on the coriander and toss to mix thoroughly.

Pour Dressing over the corn mixture and toss to coat. Cover the bowl and refrigerate for at least two hours.

Dressing
1/3 cup vegetable oil
2 tablespoons white wine vinegar
1/2 teaspoon Dijon mustard

1/2 teaspoon salt
1/8 teaspoon paprika

In a small bowl whisk together all the ingredients.

ndive and Grapefruit Salad

6 endive

3 pink grapefruit

watercress sprigs for garnish

Remove about 20 of the largest outer leaves from the endive being careful not to tear the leaves. Set aside. Cut remaining endive crosswise into 1/2-inch pieces and transfer to large bowl.

Peel grapefruit with a sharp knife and remove the peel and pith. Do this over a bowl to catch the juice. Reserve the juice. Cut the grapefruit along membrane and carefully remove segments, then cut into 1/2-inch pieces. Add to the endive. Toss lightly, cover and refrigerate.

To serve:

Arrange reserved endive leaves in a fan pattern with flat ends meeting at center. Mound the grapefruit mixture over top and drizzle the Dressing over the salad. Garnish with watercress sprigs.

Dressing

3 tablespoons of the reserved
   grapefruit juice

6 tablespoons walnut oil

1 teaspoon lemon juice

3/4 teaspoon Dijon mustard

1/4 teaspoon salt

white pepper to taste

In a small bowl combine the reserved grapefruit juice with the oil, lemon juice, mustard, salt and pepper. Whisk until well blended. Adjust seasoning, if necessary.

6 servings

Lentil and Sausage Salad

1 cup lentils
4 cups water
6 ounces smoked kielbasa, peeled
  and thinly sliced
1/2 cup chopped red onion
3 tablespoons chopped fresh
  parsley

12 pitted black olives, quartered
1/2 cup chopped cooked carrots
1 1/2 teaspoons Dijon mustard
2 tablespoons red wine vinegar
1/4 cup olive oil
salt and pepper to taste

In a large saucepan bring lentils and water to a boil. Cover, lower heat and simmer until lentils are just tender, about 40 minutes. Drain and set aside, covered.

In a large bowl combine the sausage, onion, parsley, olives and carrots.

In another bowl combine the mustard and vinegar, stirring until smooth. Add the olive oil and beat until well blended.

Pour half the dressing over the sausage mixture. Add the lentils. Add the remaining dressing. Adjust seasoning with salt and pepper.

4 to 6 servings

Lettuce and Bacon Salad

1 large head iceberg lettuce, torn
  in pieces
1 red onion, chopped
4 hard-cooked eggs, chopped
a 10-ounce package frozen petit
  peas, thawed

2/3 cup mayonnaise
1/3 cup sour cream
2 teaspoons sugar
1 cup grated Parmesan cheese
8 slices cooked bacon, crumbled

Must be prepared a day in advance.

In a large serving bowl layer the lettuce, onion, eggs and petit peas.

In a small bowl combine the mayonnaise and sour cream and spread on top of the vegetables.

In another bowl mix together the sugar, Parmesan cheese and bacon. Sprinkle over all. Cover bowl with plastic wrap and refrigerate overnight.

Before serving, toss the salad to combine.

8 servings

Papaya, Jerusalem Artichoke and Avocado Salad

2 papayas, peeled, halved
   lengthwise, seeded and sliced
   crosswise
2 avocados, peeled, pitted, cubed,
   and sprinkled with lemon juice

2 Jerusalem artichokes, peeled,
   cut into matchstick pieces, and
   tossed with 1/8 cup lime juice
Honey Lime Dressing
sprigs of coriander for garnish

Arrange the papaya on a serving platter and mound the avocado over it. Drain the Jerusalem artichokes and sprinkle them over the mixture.

Drizzle the Honey Lime Dressing over the salad and garnish with the coriander.

Honey Lime Dressing
1 tablespoon honey
1/8 cup lime juice or to taste

salt and pepper to taste
1/4 cup olive oil or to taste

In a bowl combine the honey, lime juice, and salt and pepper. Slowly whisk in the oil in a steady stream.

6 servings

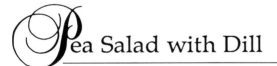Pea Salad with Dill

1 cup fresh snow peas, julienned
two 10-ounce packages frozen
   petit peas, thawed
1/3 cup sour cream

1/3 cup mayonnaise
1/2 cup chopped fresh dill
salt and pepper to taste
4 slices cooked bacon, crumbled

In a saucepan bring water to a boil and blanch the snow peas 30 to 60 seconds. Drain.

In a small bowl combine the sour cream, mayonnaise, dill and salt and pepper. Add the peas mixing lightly. Cover and refrigerate for 30 minutes. Adjust seasoning with salt and pepper.

Transfer to a glass serving bowl and sprinkle the bacon over all.

10 servings

ice Salad

4 cups rice
4 ginger slices
2 teaspoons salt
pepper to taste
1/2 teaspoon cumin or to taste
1 cup golden raisins
1/4 cup olive oil

1 tablespoon lemon juice or to
taste
1 cup slivered almonds, blanched
1 cup dried apricots or prunes or
combined to equal 1 cup (soaked
in boiling water for 10 minutes,
drained and chopped)
1 cup chopped scallions

In a saucepan bring 8 cups of water to a boil and add the rice and ginger. Cover and cook until rice is tender but still firm, about 20 minutes. Remove ginger slices and set aside. Drain rice in a sieve and transfer to a large bowl. Add the salt, pepper, cumin, raisins and oil. Stir in the lemon juice. Mince the ginger slices and mix with the rice.

When salad is cool add the almonds, apricots and scallions. Serve at room temperature.

16 servings

urried Rice Salad

1 1/2 cups rice
3 cups chicken broth
1/2 cup julienne carrots
1 teaspoon curry powder
1/4 teaspoon cumin
1/4 teaspoon minced garlic
3 tablespoons grated radish
2 tablespoons pine nuts, toasted

2 tablespoons lime juice
1 tablespoon red wine vinegar
2 tablespoons vegetable oil
1 tablespoon chopped fresh
parsley
1 teaspoon minced fresh dill
2 scallions, thinly sliced
2 tablespoons chutney

In a saucepan cook the rice in the broth until tender, about 20 minutes. Drain and place the rice in a serving bowl. Let cool.

Combine all the remaining ingredients and toss with the rice. Serve at room temperature.

8 servings

# Potato Salad

8-10 medium potatoes, cooked,
   cooled, peeled and sliced
2 hard-cooked eggs

2 large red onions, sliced
celery seed to taste

Must be prepared in advance.

Separate the yolks from the whites of the hard-cooked eggs. Slice the egg whites thinly.

In a serving bowl layer the potatoes, onions and egg whites. Sprinkle with celery seed. Pour Dressing on top. Cover and refrigerate, stirring once or twice, for several hours.

Dressing
1 cup olive oil
1 tablespoon salt
1 teaspoon pepper
2 tablespoons sugar

2 teaspoons dry mustard
1/2 cup vinegar
1 egg
salt and pepper to taste

In a bowl mash the egg yolks and mix with 1/2 cup of the oil. Add the salt, pepper and sugar. Set aside.

In another bowl combine the dry mustard with 2 tablespoons of the vinegar . Add to the egg yolk mixture.

In a separate bowl beat together the remaining 1/2 cup oil and the rest of the vinegar with the 1 egg. Add to the egg yolk mixture. Adjust seasoning with salt and pepper.

8 to 10 servings

New Potatoes with Peas and Mint

20 small new red potatoes, rinsed
1/3 cup olive oil
1/2 cup white wine
2 cups fresh peas
2 cups crème fraîche

1/2 cup chopped fresh mint
3 tablespoons chopped fresh
  chives
salt and pepper to taste

Must be prepared in advance.

In a saucepan boil the potatoes in water to cover until tender. Drain. Cut into quarters, leaving skins on, while still hot. Transfer to a large bowl.

In a small bowl whisk the oil and wine together and pour over the hot potatoes. Stir to coat well. Let cool to room temperature.

Add the peas, crème fraîche, mint and chives. Toss gently to blend. Cover and refrigerate two to three hours.

Before serving, adjust seasoning with salt and pepper.

8 servings

Romaine with Watercress Dressing

2 medium heads romaine lettuce
1 bunch radishes

1/2 teaspoon salt
Watercress Dressing

Must be prepared in advance.

Wash the romaine and spin dry. Refrigerate until crisp.

Slice radishes paper thin, place in a small bowl filled with water and refrigerate.

Before serving, tear romaine into bite-size pieces and place in a salad bowl. Drain the radishes and toss with the romaine lettuce and salt. Pour the Watercress Dressing over all and toss well.

Watercress Dressing
9 tablespoons olive oil
juice of 1 lemon
1 tablespoon tarragon vinegar
1/2 teaspoon salt

1/8 teaspoon dry mustard
1/8 teaspoon sugar
1 bunch watercress

Remove the coarse stems from the watercress and chop. In a small bowl combine the remaining ingredients and stir in the chopped watercress. Chill.

6 to 8 servings

Spinach and Endive Salad

two 10-ounce packages fresh
  spinach, rinsed, stems removed
  and spun dry
2 large endive, trimmed and
  sliced thinly crosswise

1/2 cup chopped walnuts, toasted
  lightly
Blue Cheese Walnut Dressing

In a salad bowl toss the spinach, endive, and 3 tablespoons of the walnuts with the Blue Cheese Walnut Dressing until well combined.

Blue Cheese Walnut Dressing
1/4 cup red wine vinegar
1/2 cup olive oil

2 ounces crumbled blue cheese
salt and pepper to taste

In a food processor combine the vinegar, oil, blue cheese, remaining walnuts and salt and pepper. Mix the dressing until it is smooth.

6 servings

Tomato and Hearts of Palm Salad

1/2 pound spinach, trimmed, rinsed, and dried
1 large head of Bibb lettuce, separated into leaves, rinsed and dried
4 tomatoes, cored and cut into wedges

a 14-ounce can hearts of palm, drained and cut into 1-inch pieces
1 cup oil-cured olives
Basil Vinaigrette

In a bowl toss the spinach and Bibb lettuce with the Basil Vinaigrette, reserving 1 tablespoon.

Line a large platter with the spinach and the lettuce. Arrange the tomatoes and the hearts of palm in the center over the greens and sprinkle the salad with the olives. Drizzle the remaining tablespoon of vinaigrette over all.

Basil Vinaigrette
3 tablespoons white wine vinegar
2 teaspoons Dijon mustard
1 clove garlic, minced

salt and pepper to taste
1/2 cup olive oil
2 tablespoons minced fresh basil

In a bowl combine the vinegar, mustard, garlic and salt and pepper. Whisk in the oil in a steady stream and stir in the basil.

4 servings

100

Tomatoes and Onions

3 large tomatoes, cored and
   thickly sliced

1 large Bermuda onion, cut into
   thick slices
Gorgonzola Dressing

On an oval serving platter arrange alternate and slightly overlapping slices of tomatoes and onion. Pour the Gorgonzola Dressing over all.

Gorgonzola Dressing
1 tablespoon red wine vinegar
3 tablespoons olive oil
salt and pepper to taste

4 ounces Gorgonzola cheese, room
   temperature

In a mixing bowl combine the vinegar, oil, salt and pepper and blend well. Add the cheese and cut it into the dressing. The dressing should be slightly lumpy.

4 servings

Tomato, Mozzarella and Basil Salad

4 large beefsteak tomatoes, each
   cut into 4 to 6 slices
1/2 pound mozzarella cheese, cut
   into same number of slices as
   tomatoes

10–14 fresh basil leaves
1/4 cup olive oil
salt and pepper to taste

On an oval serving platter arrange the tomatoes, mozzarella cheese and basil leaves in alternating layers, overlapping slightly. Drizzle olive oil on top and season with salt and pepper.
Serve at room temperature.

4 servings

Dressings for Green Salads, Pasta Salads and Vegetables

GREEN SALADS: Toss with dressing and serve immediately.

PASTA SALADS: Cook pasta in lightly salted water, al dente. Drain and cool under cold running water. Pat dry with paper towels and toss with desired dressing.

VEGETABLES: Cook vegetables until crisp tender. Raw vegetables may also be used. Marinate vegetables one hour at room temperature or longer in the refrigerator.

Basil Vinaigrette

1/2 teaspoon crushed garlic
1/2 teaspoon Dijon mustard
3 tablespoon red wine vinegar
1 tablespoon balsamic vinegar

1/2 cup olive oil
4 teaspoons fresh basil
salt and pepper to taste

In a food processor puree the garlic with the mustard and vinegars. Gradually add the oil. Add the basil and process until basil is finely chopped. Add salt and pepper.

Chili Vinaigrette

2 tablespoons balsamic vinegar
1 tablespoon Dijon mustard
1 shallot, minced
1 teaspoon egg yolk

1/3 cup chili sauce
1/2 cup olive oil
1/2 cup safflower oil
salt and pepper to taste

In a small bowl combine the vinegar, mustard, shallot, egg yolk and chili sauce. Whisk until well mixed.
Combine the oils and add to the vinegar mixture in a steady stream, whisking constantly. Adjust seasoning with salt and pepper.

Mustard Chive Dressing

1/4 cup Dijon mustard
1 large egg yolk
3 tablespoons lemon juice
1 clove garlic, minced

1 cup olive oil
1/4 cup chopped fresh chives or
  other fresh herbs
salt and pepper to taste

In a small bowl mix together the mustard, egg yolk, lemon juice and garlic. Add the oil in a steady stream, whisking continuously until well combined.
Stir in the chives and adjust seasoning with salt and pepper.

Lemon Tahini Sauce

1 1/2 cups buttermilk
1/2 cup lemon juice
1/2 cup Japanese soy sauce
3/4 cup safflower oil
2 scallions, chopped
1 clove garlic
1 tablespoon chopped onion

1 1/2 stalks of celery, chopped
1/2 cup minced fresh parsley
1/4 cup chopped green pepper
1/2 cucumber, peeled, seeded and
    chopped
pepper to taste
1 cup tahini (sesame seed paste)

In a food processor mix all the ingredients except the tahini. Add the tahini and blend until mixture is smooth and thick.

Herb Vinaigrette

1/2 cup olive oil
1/2 cup vegetable oil
2 tablespoons wine vinegar
2 tablespoons lemon juice
1/2 teaspoon salt
3 tablespoons Japanese soy sauce

2 tablespoons grated Parmesan
    cheese
1 teaspoon dry mustard powder
1 teaspoon rosemary
1 teaspoon thyme
2 cloves garlic

Place all the ingredients in a blender and mix for 2 to 3 minutes. Transfer to a jar, cover and refrigerate.
This vinaigrette improves with time and keeps indefinitely in the refrigerator.

Oriental Dressing

3 tablespoons sugar
3 tablespoons soy sauce
2 cloves garlic, minced
1 teaspoon minced fresh ginger
2 tablespoons Chinese red vinegar
2 tablespoons white vinegar

2 scallions, finely chopped
12 Szechuan peppercorns
dash of hot oil
few drops of sesame oil
1 tomato, chopped

Combine all the ingredients except the tomato and mix well. Before serving, add the tomato.

Sesame Dressing

2 cloves garlic, minced
1/4 cup rice vinegar
2 tablespoons sesame oil
1 tablespoon soy sauce

1/2 teaspoon sugar
pinch red pepper flakes
1 tablespoon sesame seeds,
    toasted

Combine all the ingredients except the sesame seeds and mix well until blended.
Before serving, sprinkle with the sesame seeds.

Zucchini, Yellow Squash and Romaine

1 1/2 pounds small zucchini, cut
  into 2x1/4-inch julienne
1 1/2 pounds yellow summer
  squash, cut into 2x1/4-inch
  julienne

1 large head romaine lettuce
salt and pepper to taste
Rosemary Vinaigrette

    In a large pot of boiling water blanch the zucchini and yellow squash until crisp tender, about 1 1/2 minutes. Drain and rinse with cold running water. Pat dry. *(Can be made in advance up to this point.)*

    Line a serving platter with large outer romaine leaves. Cut out tough center stems from remaining romaine. Cut leaves into 2x1/2-inch strips.

    In a bowl mix the zucchini, yellow squash and 1/2 cup of the Rosemary Vinaigrette. Let marinate 10 minutes. Mix in romaine strips and enough vinaigrette to coat. Add salt and pepper. Mound salad in the center of the prepared platter.

Rosemary Vinaigrette
2 tablespoons balsamic vinegar
1 1/2 teaspoons Dijon mustard
3/4 teaspoon salt

1/2 cup olive oil
1 teaspoon dried rosemary,
  crumbled

    In a bowl combine the vinegar, mustard and salt. Slowly whisk in the oil in a thin stream. Stir in the rosemary.

8 servings

Vegetables

A FORMAL DINNER FOR FOUR

Westport is rich in history, made all the richer from the diversity of those who have made it home. Each resident brings a heritage to the town that is reflected in their homes and the way they entertain. The table setting in this picture belongs to a Westport Young Woman's League member who counts among her most prized possessions her grandmother's Tiffany tableware. The loving care with which she sets her table reflects her pride in family history and her love for fine china.

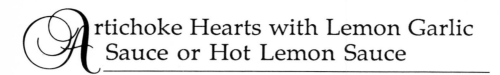

Artichoke Hearts with Lemon Garlic Sauce or Hot Lemon Sauce

4 artichokes
1/2 lemon
juice of 1 lemon

salt and pepper to taste
Lemon Garlic Sauce or
Hot Lemon Sauce

Cut off the artichoke stems and rub them with the 1/2 lemon. Cut the prickly points off the leaves and rub again with the lemon.

In a saucepan large enough to hold the artichokes in one layer, add enough water to reach a third of the way up. Add the lemon juice and salt and pepper and bring to a boil. Lower heat and simmer, covered, until tender, about 25 minutes.

Serve with Lemon Garlic Sauce or Hot Lemon Sauce.

Lemon Garlic Sauce
4 tablespoons olive oil
2 teaspoons minced garlic
2 tablespoons minced parsley

2 tablespoons lemon juice
salt and pepper to taste

In a small saucepan heat the oil and sauté the garlic for 1 minute. Do not allow to brown. Remove the saucepan from the heat, stir in the parsley and lemon juice. Adjust seasoning with salt and pepper. Serve in individual bowls.

Hot Lemon Sauce
4 tablespoons lemon juice
2 tablespoons cornstarch
1 cup chicken broth

1 tablespoon chopped fresh dill,
  parsley or other herb

In a saucepan combine the lemon juice, cornstarch and broth and whisking constantly, heat until the sauce is thickened and smooth. Stir in the dill. Pour over the warm artichokes.

4 servings

The following vegetables can be substituted for the artichoke hearts.

roccoli Rabe

1 1/2 pounds broccoli rabe

Rinse and discard any yellow leaves and coarse stem ends.

Cook the broccoli rabe with just the water clinging to the leaves, stirring occasionally, until the stems are just tender.

Toss with the Lemon Garlic Sauce or pour Hot Lemon Sauce over all.

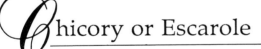russels Sprouts

a 10-ounce package of fresh
    Brussels sprouts

Remove the tough leaves and trim the stems from the Brussels sprouts. Cut a deep X in the stem end of each sprout or cut in half, if sprouts are large.

Cook, uncovered, in lightly salted water until just tender, about 10 to 15 minutes.

hicory or Escarole

1 head chicory or escarole

Cut the chicory across into 1-inch strips. Rinse in several changes of water.

In a saucepan combine the chicory with 1/2 cup water and cook, uncovered, stirring occasionally, until wilted and tender, about 10 minutes.

andelion Greens

2 pounds dandelion greens

Trim and wash the dandelion greens well. Stack the greens into bunches and cut into 1-inch lengths. Cook in lightly salted boiling water until tender, about 10 minutes.

Green Beans with Dill

1 1/2 pounds green beans, trimmed	2 tablespoons lemon juice
4 tablespoons (1/2 stick) unsalted butter *sliced fresh mushrooms*	1 tablespoon chopped fresh dill
	salt and pepper to taste

In a saucepan cook the green beans in lightly salted water uncovered, until tender but still crisp, about 5 minutes. Remove beans, drain and rinse under cold running water. Pat dry with paper towels. *mushrooms+*

In a saucepan melt the butter and add the beans. Stir fry over medium high heat until beans are heated through. Add lemon juice, dill, salt and pepper and toss to mix. Serve immediately.

6 servings

Cabbage, Potato and Apple Bake

1 medium cabbage, thinly sliced	8 tablespoons (1 stick) unsalted butter
3 baking potatoes, peeled and thinly sliced	salt and pepper to taste
3 tart green apples, peeled, cored and thinly sliced	1 cup heavy cream
1 onion, finely chopped	1/4 cup fine bread crumbs
	1/4 cup grated Swiss cheese

Preheat oven to 350°. Butter a 3-quart deep baking dish.

Layer a third each of the cabbage, potatoes, apples and onion in the prepared baking dish. Dot each layer with butter and sprinkle with salt and pepper. Repeat layering two more times. Pour the cream over the top. Cover and bake for 45 minutes.

Remove from the oven, sprinkle with the bread crumbs and Swiss cheese. Return to the oven, uncovered, until cheese is melted and lightly browned.

6 servings

Carrots with Ginger and Lime

3 cups water
1 1/2 teaspoons salt
3 pounds carrots, cut diagonally
   into 1/4-inch slices
3 tablespoons unsalted butter

2 tablespoons honey
2 tablespoons fresh lime juice
1 tablespoon grated lime rind
1 tablespoon minced fresh ginger
lime slices for garnish

In a saucepan bring the water to a boil, add salt and carrots. Lower heat and simmer, uncovered, until tender but still crisp, about 8 minutes. Drain and return carrots to the saucepan

Meanwhile, in another saucepan, melt the butter, add the honey, lime juice, lime rind and ginger and slowly bring to a boil. Remove from heat.

Pour sauce over carrots. Warm over low heat, stirring constantly, until carrots are glazed, about 2 minutes.

Garnish with lime slices.

6 servings

Carrots and Chick Peas

1 1/3 cups chicken broth
2 carrots, thinly sliced
an 8-ounce can chick peas or
   kidney beans, drained and
   rinsed
1/2 cup barley

1 small onion, chopped
1/4 cup chopped fresh parsley
3 tablespoons bulghur
1/8 teaspoon garlic powder
2 ounces cheddar cheese,
   shredded

Preheat oven to 350°.

In a 1-quart casserole combine the chicken broth, carrots, chick peas, barley, onion, parsley, bulghur, and garlic powder.

Cover and bake until the barley and carrots are just tender, about 50 minutes.

Sprinkle the Cheddar cheese on top. Bake until cheese melts, 2 to 3 minutes longer.

4 to 6 servings

Carrots and Cauliflower with Dill

2 tablespoons unsalted butter
1 teaspoon sugar
1/2 teaspoon salt
white pepper to taste
1/4 cup water
1 small head of cauliflower, cut
into 1-inch florets

6 carrots, cut into 2-inch julienne
strips
3 tablespoons finely chopped
fresh dill plus dill sprigs for
garnish

In a saucepan melt the butter with the sugar, salt, white pepper and water. Add the cauliflower and simmer, covered, stirring occasionally, until it is just tender, about 10 to 12 minutes. Transfer the cauliflower with a slotted spoon to the center of a serving plate and keep it warm.

In the same saucepan, add the carrots, cover and simmer, stirring occasionally, until they are just tender, about 5 minutes. Transfer the carrots with a slotted spoon to the serving plate, arranging them around the cauliflower and spoon any pan juices over the vegetables.

Sprinkle the vegetables with the chopped dill and salt and pepper to taste.

Garnish with the dill sprigs.

4 servings

Corn with Basil

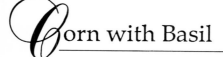

2 tablespoons unsalted butter
2 tablespoons vegetable oil
1 red pepper, seeded and coarsely
chopped
2 tablespoons chopped chives
two 10-ounce packages frozen
corn, thawed

1/2 cup water
1 tablespoon chopped fresh basil
1 teaspoon sugar
1/4 teaspoon salt
black pepper to taste

In a saucepan melt the butter with the oil. Add the pepper and chives and cook for 1 minute. Stir in the corn and cook 1 minute longer. Add the water, bring to a boil, lower heat, cover and simmer until the corn is tender, about 5 minutes.

Sprinkle on the basil, sugar, salt and pepper. Stir over high heat until all the liquid is evaporated.

4 servings

Roasted Corn with Curry Butter

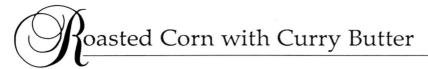

1 1/4 teaspoons curry powder
8 tablespoons (1 stick) unsalted
  butter, softened

6 ears corn, husks and silk
  removed
salt and pepper to taste

Preheat oven to 400°.

In a small bowl combine the butter and curry powder. Spread over the corn and sprinkle with salt and pepper.

Wrap individually in aluminum foil and close ends to seal tightly. Place on oven rack and cook 25 to 30 minutes.

6 servings

Eggplant Parmesan

1 large eggplant (about 2 pounds),
  peeled and cut into 1/2-inch
  thick slices
3 tablespoons flour
1/2 teaspoon salt
1/2-3/4 cup olive oil
a 6-ounce can tomato paste
1 cup water

1 clove garlic, crushed
1 teaspoon dried oregano
1/4 teaspoon dried basil
1/4 teaspoon pepper
6 ounces Genoa salami, sliced
6 ounces mozzarella cheese, sliced
6 ounces grated Parmesan cheese

Preheat oven to 350°. Oil a 10-inch square baking dish.

Season flour with salt and coat the eggplant slices. In a skillet heat the oil and brown eggplant on both sides over medium high heat. Drain on paper towels and set aside.

Meanwhile, in a saucepan combine the tomato paste, water, garlic, oregano, basil and pepper and simmer 30 minutes.

Arrange half of the eggplant slices on the bottom of the baking dish. Cover with half of the tomato sauce and half each of the salami the mozzarella cheese and Parmesan cheese. Repeat.

Bake for 25 to 30 minutes or until the cheese is melted and lightly browned.

4 servings

Baked Eggplant with Tomato

1 large eggplant (about 2 pounds),
  peeled and sliced
1 1/2 teaspoons salt
2 eggs, beaten
2 tablespoons unsalted butter,
  melted
coarsely ground black pepper

3 tablespoons chopped onion
1/2 teaspoon dried oregano
3/4 cup seasoned bread crumbs
6 ounces Colby cheese, grated
4 ounces grated Parmesan cheese
2 large tomatoes sliced in thirds
paprika to taste

Preheat oven to 375°. Oil a shallow 1-1/2 quart baking dish.

In a small saucepan combine the eggplant with the salt and about 1 inch of boiling water. Cover tightly and cook 10 minutes. Drain.

In a bowl mash the eggplant and mix with the eggs, butter, pepper, onion, oregano and bread crumbs. Set aside.

Mix the cheeses together.

Cover the bottom of the baking dish with half of the tomatoes and a third of the cheese mixture. Cover with half of the eggplant mixture. Repeat. Top with remaining cheese mixture. Sprinkle with paprika. Cover and bake for 45 minutes.

4 to 6 servings

Leek and Tomatoes

1/3 cup olive oil
2 large onions, thinly sliced
1 clove garlic, minced
2 pounds leeks (white part only),
  washed well and cut
  lengthwise into 2-inch pieces

2 tomatoes, peeled and thinly
  sliced
salt and white pepper to taste
1/2 cup water

In a saucepan heat the oil and sauté the onion with the garlic until the onion is golden brown. Add the leeks, tomatoes and salt and pepper. Mix in the water and simmer, covered, for 1/2 hour, stirring occasionally.

4 servings

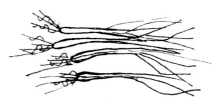

Baked Mushrooms and Barley

5 tablespoons unsalted butter
3/4 pound mushrooms, sliced
1 large onion, chopped

1 cup barley
2 cups beef broth

Preheat oven to 350°.

In a saucepan melt the butter and sauté the mushrooms and onion until the mushroom juices evaporate and the onion is softened. Add the barley and cook until lightly browned.

Transfer to a baking dish. Add 1 cup of the broth, cover and bring to a boil. Set baking dish in the oven and bake for 25 to 30 minutes. Add remaining broth. Continue to cook, covered, until liquid is absorbed and barley is tender, about 15 minutes longer.

4 to 6 servings

Honey Glazed Onions with Mint

2 tablespoons butter
1 1/2 pounds pearl onions, peeled
1 clove garlic, crushed
1 tablespoon honey

1 cup chicken broth
1 tablespoon chopped fresh mint
    or 1 teaspoon dried mint

In a heavy skillet large enough to hold the onions in a single layer melt the butter. Add the onions and garlic and sauté until golden. Discard the garlic.

In a bowl mix the honey and broth and pour over the onions. Bring to a boil, lower heat and simmer until almost all the liquid has evaporated and the onions are tender, about 30 minutes. Stir in the mint.

4 servings

nions and Mushrooms

2 pounds mushrooms, stems
  removed
12 tablespoons (1 1/2 sticks)
  unsalted butter, melted
1 tablespoon dried thyme

1 tablespoon chopped fresh
  parsley
1/8 cup red wine vinegar
salt and pepper to taste
Roasted Onions

Preheat oven to 450°.

In a small bowl combine the butter, thyme and parsley. Add the mushroom caps and mix well.

Place the mushroom caps in a double layer in a baking dish. Sprinkle on top the vinegar, salt and pepper. Bake for 15 minutes. Remove from oven and stir in the Roasted Onions, basting well. Bake 10 minutes longer.

Roasted Onions
1/2 pound onions, cut into 1/2-inch
  thick rings

4 tablespoons unsalted butter,
  melted

Preheat oven to 450°.

Combine onions with the butter and bake, turning occasionally until cooked, about 25 minutes.

4 to 6 servings

ried Parsley

sprigs of parsley
oil for frying

salt

Wash sprigs of parsley well. Dry thoroughly with paper towels.

In a heavy saucepan heat the oil and toss in the parsley sprigs, a few at a time. Remove with a slotted spoon as soon as they rise to the surface, about one to two minutes. Season lightly with salt. Serve immediately.

Black-eyed Peas

a 1-pound can black-eyed peas,
  partially drained
2 slices bacon
1 cup chopped onion
1/4 cup chopped green pepper

1 cup chopped celery
a 14-ounce can tomatoes with juice
1 teaspoon sugar
1 bay leaf

Preheat oven to 350°.

In a skillet cook the bacon until crisp. Remove the bacon and in the drippings sauté the onion, pepper and celery until tender. Chop the bacon and add to the onion mixture. Add the tomatoes, sugar, and bay leaf and stir well. Simmer for 5 minutes.
  Add the peas and mix thoroughly. Transfer to a 1-quart baking dish. Bake for 30 minutes or until most of the liquid is absorbed.

6 servings

Snow Peas with Sesame Seeds

1 pound fresh snow peas, strings
  removed
1 tablespoon soy sauce
1 1/2 teaspoons finely chopped
  fresh ginger

1 clove garlic, minced
1 1/2 tablespoons sesame oil
1 tablespoon sesame seeds,
  toasted

In a small bowl combine the soy sauce, ginger and garlic. Set aside.
  In a saucepan heat the oil over medium high heat. Add the snow peas and soy sauce mixture and stir fry for 1 minute. Cover and cook the snow peas until just tender, about 1 to 2 minutes. Stir in the sesame seeds.

4 servings

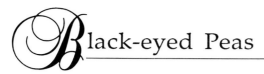

$\mathcal{P}$eppers Stuffed with Rice

6 green or red peppers
1/4 cup oil
2 large onions, finely chopped
1 cup plus 2 tablespoons enriched
 white rice
1/2 cup hot water

4 ounces tomato sauce
1/2 cup finely chopped fresh dill
dash of allspice
1/2 cup currants
1 teaspoon salt
pepper to taste

Preheat oven to 350°.

Cut a 1/4-inch slice from the stem end of each pepper and remove the seeds and membranes. Reserve the tops. Rinse the peppers to remove all the seeds. Lightly salt the inside of each pepper and turn upside down to drain.

In a saucepan heat the oil and sauté the onion until very soft and lightly browned. Add the rice and stir continuously until the rice is opaque. Mix in the hot water, tomato sauce, dill, allspice, currants and salt and pepper. Cover and cook for 5 minutes.

Spoon the rice filling lightly into peppers. Cover peppers with the reserved tops and secure with toothpicks.

Arrange peppers in a single layer in a baking pan large enough to hold the peppers close together in one layer. Add 2 1/2 cups water to the baking pan. Cover with foil. Bake for 1/2 hour. Remove foil, baste peppers with the pan liquids.

Increase oven temperature to 375°. Continue baking, uncovered, for 1/2 hour longer, basting occasionally and adding more water, if necessary.

Serve warm or at room temperature.

Can be made in advance.

6 servings

ℬaked Garden Vegetables

8-10 boiling potatoes (about 3 pounds) cut into 1/8-inch thin slices
3/4 cup olive oil, approximately
1/4 cup chopped parsley
1 large red pepper
2 large green peppers
2 carrots, sliced thinly on the diagonal

4 tomatoes, chopped
3-4 small zucchini (1 to 1 1/2 pounds), cut into 1/2-inch thick slices
2 large red onions, cut into half-round slices
20-24 black Kalamata olives, pitted
salt and pepper to taste

Preheat oven to 375°. Oil a 9x12-inch baking dish.

Arrange potatoes in a 1/2-inch thick layer on the bottom of the baking dish. Sprinkle the potatoes very lightly with salt and pepper and a few drops of olive oil.
Cut all peppers in half lengthwise, remove seeds, then cut into thin, half-round strips.
Arrange all the vegetables except the olives in layers on top of the potatoes, alternating with the parsley and sprinkling with the salt and pepper. Layer sparsely to create rows of colors.
When all the vegetables are arranged, distribute olives evenly over the top and press them down gently. (If canned olives are used, adjust seasoning with more salt.) Drizzle about half a cup of olive oil over the top. Cover and bake for 25 minutes. Remove cover and continue baking for about 2 hours or until all the vegetables are cooked. If vegetables seem dry, brush with oil or cover again for a few more minutes.
Serve directly from the dish, scooping up the potato base with the other vegetables.

8 to 10 servings

Potatoes Stuffed with Chilies and Cheese

6 baking potatoes, scrubbed and
   patted dry
2 tablespoons vegetable oil
1 cup grated Monterey Jack cheese

a 4-ounce can chopped hot green
   chili peppers, drained
1/3 cup sour cream
2 large eggs, beaten lightly
salt and pepper to taste

Preheat oven to 425°.

Rub the potatoes with the oil and bake for 30 minutes. Prick them with a fork and continue baking for 1/2 hour more.

Cut a lengthwise slice from the top of each potato. Scoop out the pulp leaving 1/2-inch thick shells and force through a ricer into a large bowl. Beat in 2/3 cup of the Monterey Jack cheese, the chili peppers, sour cream, eggs, and salt and pepper to taste and beat the mixture until it is fluffy.

Mound the filling in the shells and sprinkle with the remaining 1/3 cup Monterey Jack cheese. (*Can be made in advance up to this point.*)

Place the potatoes on a baking sheet and bake for 10 minutes.

6 servings

Pan Roasted Potatoes

6 medium all-purpose potatoes,
   peeled
1 onion, sliced thinly
4 tablespoons (1/2 stick) unsalted
   butter, melted

2 tablespoons olive oil
garlic powder to taste
salt and pepper to taste

Preheat oven to 400°.

Cut potatoes haphazardly into 2-inch chunks. Place potatoes in a saucepan and cover with water. Bring to a boil, lower heat and cook 1 minute. Drain. Place potatoes in baking pan just large enough to hold them in one layer. Mix in the onion.

In a bowl combine the butter and oil. Pour over the potatoes and onion and toss until well coated. Sprinkle with the garlic powder and salt and pepper.

Bake, uncovered, turning occasionally until browned and crisp on the outside, about 30 minutes.

6 servings

# Rösti Potatoes

6 large boiling potatoes (about 2 pounds)	salt and pepper to taste
1/2 cup clarified butter	1 tablespoon lightly salted butter, softened

Must be prepared a day in advance.

Cook the potatoes in lightly salted water until barely tender but not cooked through, about 10 minutes. Drain and refrigerate overnight.

Peel and coarsely grate the potatoes, using a grater or the shredding disk of a food processor.

In a 10-inch skillet heat the clarified butter until quite hot. Spread half the potatoes in the pan and season with salt and pepper. Cover with the remaining potatoes and cook over medium high heat until the bottom is brown and crusty, about 10 to 12 minutes.

Flip the pancake over by placing an inverted plate on the skillet, turning both together so the pancake is on the plate, then slipping the pancake back into the skillet.

Cook the rösti until the other side is browned, about 7 to 10 minutes longer, sprinkle with salt and pepper and gloss with the softened butter. Transfer the rösti to a round serving plate and cut into wedges.

6 to 8 servings

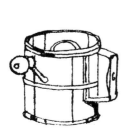
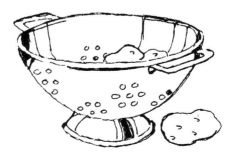

Sweet Potatoes with Pecans

6 sweet potatoes or yams
8 tablespoons (1 stick) unsalted
  butter, melted
1/2-3/4 cup maple syrup

1/2 cup coarsely chopped pecans
1/4 cup golden raisins
brown sugar to taste

Preheat oven to 350°.

Bake the sweet potatoes until they are tender, about 1 hour. Let cool. *Can be prepared up to a day in advance.*

Preheat oven to 375°. Butter a shallow 2-quart baking dish.

Peel the potatoes and cut them into eighths. Place in the baking dish.

In a small bowl combine the butter, maple syrup, pecans and raisins and pour over the potatoes. Toss to mix well. Sprinkle top with brown sugar.

Bake, uncovered, for 20 to 30 minutes. Do not allow the potatoes to dry out. Add more butter, if necessary.

When cooked, broil about 4 inches from the heat until the edges of the potatoes are browned lightly.

6 to 8 servings

Rice with Saffron

2 cups rice
4 tablespoons unsalted butter
1 medium onion, chopped
1 teaspoon saffron threads

3 1/2 cups chicken broth
3 tablespoons chopped pistachio
  nuts

In a saucepan melt the butter and sauté the onion until soft, about 5 minutes. Stir in the saffron and cook 1 minute longer. Add the rice and toss to coat.

Add the chicken broth. Bring to a boil, lower heat, cover and simmer until liquid is absorbed and rice is cooked, about 25 minutes. Stir in the pistachio nuts.

6 to 8 servings

Curried Rice

3 tablespoons unsalted butter
2 tablespoons minced onion
1/4 teaspoon minced garlic
1 cup rice

1 tablespoon curry powder
1 1/2 cups chicken broth
2 sprigs parsley
1 small bay leaf

Preheat oven to 400°.

In a saucepan, melt 1 tablespoon butter and sauté the onion and garlic, stirring until onion is softened. Add the rice and stir briefly until all the rice is coated with the butter. Transfer to a small baking dish.

Stir in the curry powder and mix well. Add the broth and stir to break up any lumps that might form. Add parsley and bay leaf. Cover and place in oven.

Bake 20 minutes. Discard parsley and bay leaf. Gently stir in remaining butter.

4 to 6 servings

Savory Baked Rice

4 tablespoons unsalted butter
1 onion, chopped
1/2 green pepper, chopped
1/2 pound mushrooms, sliced
1/4 cup chopped celery
1 cup rice

2 cups beef broth
1/2 cup slivered almonds plus 2
    tablespoons for topping, toasted
1/4 teaspoon salt
1/2 cup golden raisins (optional)

Preheat oven to 350°.

In a small saucepan melt the butter and sauté the onion, green pepper, mushrooms and celery until onion is softened.

Transfer to a 1 1/2-quart baking dish. Add the rice, broth, salt and the 1/2 cup of almonds and mix well. Cover and bake 40 to 45 minutes.

Five minutes before rice is done, add raisins, if desired. Top with additional almonds.

4 to 6 servings

LUNCHEON ON THE TERRACE

When a League member achieves national prominence it doesn't go unnoticed or unappreciated. Beverly Ellsley is such a member. Beverly Ellsley Interiors is certainly a design force that has achieved a well-deserved reputation for both decorating and remodeling work that has drawn the attention of most of the home design magazines. Beverly's design ideas are coveted by groups organizing show houses such as Kips Bay in New York.

However, Beverly Ellsley is also known to the League as a gracious hostess who lends her lovingly restored hunting-lodge home along the Saugatuck River for League Christmas parties. Though she and her family have collected many beautiful country rustic pieces, such as the twig chair in this photograph, it is probably the Ellsley's twenty-foot Victorian Christmas tree that most new members hear about first.

$\mathcal{R}$ice and Bulghur

2 tablespoons unsalted butter
1 onion, finely chopped
1/2 cup rice
1 cup bulghur

a 13 3/4-ounce can chicken broth
3 tablespoons soy sauce
6 scallions, finely chopped

In a saucepan melt the butter and sauté the onion until it is softened. Add the rice and cook, stirring until rice is transparent.

Add the bulghur, broth and soy sauce. Bring to a boil, lower heat, cover and simmer until liquid is absorbed, about 30 minutes.

Before serving, stir in the scallions.

4 servings

$\mathcal{B}$aked Rice with Tomatoes and Cheese

3 tablespoons unsalted butter
1/3 cup finely chopped onion
1 clove garlic, finely minced
1/3 cup diced tomato
1 cup rice
1/2 teaspoon dried thyme
1/2 bay leaf

1 1/3 cup chicken broth
2 tablespoons grated Parmesan
  cheese
3 tablespoons grated Gruyère
  cheese
1 tablespoon finely chopped fresh
  parsley

Preheat oven to 400°.

In a saucepan melt 1 tablespoon of the butter and sauté the onion and garlic until onion is soft and golden. Add the tomato, rice, thyme and bay leaf. Stir in the broth and bring to a boil. Transfer the rice mixture to an ovenproof baking dish and bake until all the broth is absorbed, about 18 minutes. Discard the bay leaf and gently stir in the remaining 2 tablespoons butter, Parmesan cheese, Gruyère cheese and parsley.

4 to 6 servings

$\mathscr{S}$pinach with Cognac

1 pound fresh spinach, washed
4 tablespoons unsalted butter

1 1/2 tablespoons cognac
salt and pepper to taste

In a large saucepan place the spinach with just the water cling-ing to the leaves, cover and cook briefly, stirring occasionally, being careful spinach doesn't stick to the saucepan. When wilted, drain well and return to the saucepan.

In another saucepan melt the butter and heat until it starts to brown. Pour the butter and cognac over the spinach and add salt and pepper.

4 servings

$\mathscr{B}$utternut Squash with Apple

4 tablespoons (1/2 stick) unsalted
   butter
4 large shallots, chopped
1 large leek, rinsed well and
   sliced
2 pounds butternut squash, peeled,
   seeded, quartered and sliced

1 tart green apple, peeled,
   halved, cored and sliced
1 1/2 tablespoons maple syrup
1/2 teaspoon nutmeg
1/2 cup chopped fresh parsley
salt and pepper to taste

In a large saucepan melt the butter and stir in the shallots, leek and squash. Cover and cook until crisp but still tender, about 8 minutes.

Add the apple, maple syrup, nutmeg and toss to combine. Cook until the apples soften slightly, stirring occasionally, about 4 minutes. Stir in the parsley. Adjust seasoning with salt and pepper.

6 servings

Spaghetti Squash

an 8-inch spaghetti squash
4 tablespoons unsalted butter
1 cup chopped onion
2 cloves garlic, crushed
salt and pepper to taste
1/2 pound fresh mushrooms,
 sliced
1/4 cup chopped fresh parsley

1 teaspoon dried basil
dash of dried thyme
1/2 teaspoon dried oregano
2 tomatoes, chopped
1 cup cottage or ricotta cheese
1 cup grated mozzarella cheese
1 cup fine bread crumbs
1 cup grated Parmesan cheese

Preheat oven to 375°. Butter a 2-quart baking dish.

Slice the squash in half through the middle and scoop out the seeds and fibers. Bake face down on a buttered baking sheet for about 30 minutes or until easily pierced with a fork. Let cool. Scoop out the strands of flesh.

In a saucepan melt the butter and sauté the onion and garlic with salt, pepper, mushrooms and herbs. When onions are soft, add the tomatoes. Cook until most of the liquid has evaporated.

Combine all the ingredients. Pour into prepared baking dish. Top with the Parmesan cheese. Bake, uncovered, about 40 minutes.

4 to 6 servings

Yellow Squash with Cheese

2 tablespoons olive oil
1 cup finely chopped onion
1 pound yellow squash, cut
 diagonally into 1/4-inch thick
 slices

2 tomatoes, peeled and diced
1/4 teaspoon dried thyme
salt and pepper to taste
1 cup grated Gruyère cheese

In a saucepan heat the oil and sauté the onion until it is soft. Add the squash and cook, stirring occasionally, for two minutes. Add the tomatoes, thyme and salt and pepper. Cover and cook 5 minutes. Transfer squash to a baking dish and sprinkle with the Gruyère cheese. Broil until top is golden brown, about 5 minutes.

4 servings

Stuffed Tomatoes

4 large tomatoes
3 tablespoons fresh bread crumbs, browned
1 clove garlic, minced

1 tablespoon chopped fresh parsley
salt and pepper to taste
2 tablespoons unsalted butter, melted

Preheat oven to 375°. Butter a 1-quart shallow baking dish.

Cut the tomatoes in half, squeeze out seeds and excess liquid and place in the baking dish.

In a bowl combine the bread crumbs, garlic, parsley and salt and pepper. Add the butter and mix to form a crumbly mixture. Spoon the mixture into the tomatoes. *(Can be made in advance up to this point.)*

Bake until just tender, about 12 to 15 minutes.

4 servings

Zucchini with Cherry Tomatoes

1 1/2 pounds small zucchini, cut into 1/2-inch slices
3 tablespoons unsalted butter
1 pint cherry tomatoes, cut in halves

2 teaspoons fresh lemon juice
1/4 teaspoon sugar
salt and pepper to taste

In a saucepan steam the zucchini until barely tender, about 5 minutes.

In another saucepan melt the butter and add the zucchini, tomatoes, lemon juice, sugar and salt and pepper. Toss gently to mix.

Return saucepan to heat, cover and simmer until the tomatoes are heated through, about 3 minutes.

4 to 6 servings

Zucchini Lasagne

4 tablespoons olive oil
1/2 pound ground beef or sausage
1/2 cup chopped onion
2 cloves garlic, minced
a 14-ounce can tomatoes with juice
a 6-ounce can tomato paste
1/4 pound fresh mushrooms,
  sliced
3/4 cup dry red wine

1 1/2 teaspoons dried oregano
1/4 teaspoon dried thyme
1/2 teaspoon dried basil
salt and pepper to taste
4 large zucchini
1/2 pound mozzarella cheese,
  diced
1/2 pound ricotta cheese
1/2 cup grated Parmesan cheese

Preheat oven to 350°. Butter an ovenproof serving dish.

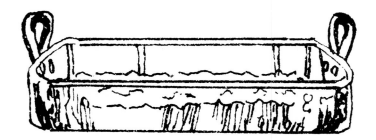

In a skillet heat 2 tablespoons of the oil and brown the meat with the onion and garlic. Add the tomatoes, tomato paste, mushrooms, wine, oregano, thyme and basil and salt and pepper. Simmer for 1/2 hour or until sauce is thickened.

Slice the zucchini lengthwise. In a skillet heat the remaining oil and lightly brown the zucchini. Combine the mozzarella and ricotta cheeses. Place a layer of zucchini in the serving dish. Add a layer of meat sauce and the combined cheeses. Continue layering, ending with the meat sauce. Sprinkle with the Parmesan cheese.

Bake for 20 to 30 minutes.
Can be made in advance.

6 servings

Seafood

Bluefish Baked in Parchment

four 1/2-pound bluefish fillets
6 tablespoons (3/4 stick) unsalted
  butter
2 tablespoons minced shallot
1/4 cup minced fresh parsley

2 teaspoons fresh lemon juice
8 baby carrots, peeled and cut in
  half lengthwise
12 lemon slices

Preheat oven to 400°.

In a small saucepan melt the butter and sauté the shallot, stirring until it is soft. Add the parsley and lemon juice.

Arrange each fillet, skin side down, on buttered parchment large enough to enclose each fillet. Pour a quarter of the sauce over each fillet, and top with 4 carrot halves and 3 lemon slices.

Fold over the parchment and crimp the edges to seal well. Bake the packets on a jelly-roll pan for 25 minutes. Transfer the packets to a serving platter.

4 servings

Crab with Shrimp

3 tablespoons unsalted butter
1 onion, minced
1/2 green pepper, finely chopped
1/2 red pepper, finely chopped
1 cup fresh bread crumbs
1 teaspoon dry mustard or to taste
1 teaspoon Worcestershire sauce

Tabasco sauce to taste
1 cup heavy cream
6 ounces lump crab meat, picked
  over
salt and pepper to taste
8 large shrimp, shelled, deveined
  and cut in half, lengthwise

Preheat oven to 400°.

In a saucepan melt the butter and sauté the onion, green pepper and red pepper, stirring occasionally until they are soft, about 5 minutes. Transfer the mixture to a bowl and add the bread crumbs, mustard, Worcestershire sauce and Tabasco sauce. Stir in the cream, crab meat and salt and pepper.

Divide the shrimp among four buttered ramekins, spoon the crab mixture over them, and bake on a baking sheet until the mixture is bubbling and the tops are golden brown, about 12 to 15 minutes.

4 servings

Rolled Fillets of Fish with Shrimp

6 fish fillets
4 tablespoons (1/2 stick) unsalted
  butter
6 shallots, finely chopped
4 cloves garlic, minced
1/2 pound shrimp, deveined,
  cooked and sliced
2 tablespoons chopped chives
1/4 cup fresh bread crumbs

6 large mushrooms, minced
1/4 cup tomato paste
salt and white pepper to taste
2 cups hot water
1/2 cup white wine
2 tablespoons lemon juice
grated Parmesan cheese
White Sauce

Preheat oven to 400°. Butter a shallow baking dish large enough to hold 4 fish rolls.

In a small saucepan melt the butter and sauté the shallots and garlic until soft, about 2 minutes. Add the shrimp. Add the chives, bread crumbs, mushrooms, tomato paste and salt and pepper.
Salt and pepper the fillets. Spread shrimp mixture on the fillets. Roll each fillet and place in the baking dish.
In a small bowl combine the water, wine and lemon juice. Pour over fish rolls. Sprinkle with the Parmesan cheese. Bake, uncovered, until tender but still moist, about 25 minutes.
Serve with White Sauce.

White Sauce
2 tablespoons unsalted butter
1 tablespoon flour
1 cup milk
1/4 cup white wine

1 tablespoon soy sauce
1/2 teaspoon salt
dash white pepper
3 egg yolks, lightly beaten

In a double boiler melt the butter and stir in the flour. Slowly add the milk. Cook, stirring, until mixture is smooth and thick. Add the wine, soy sauce and salt and pepper. Cook a few minutes. Stir in the egg yolks. Cook, stirring frequently, until sauce is thickened.

6 servings

Fillets of Fish with Spinach

2 pounds fish fillets,
  cut into 6 serving pieces
1 1/2 pounds fresh spinach, rinsed
  and chopped
4 tablespoons (1/2 stick) unsalted
  butter
2 scallions, finely chopped

1/4 cup flour
1 1/2 cups light cream
salt and pepper to taste
1/8 teaspoon nutmeg
1 teaspoon Worcestershire sauce
1/3 cup grated Gruyère cheese
1/4 cup grated Parmesan cheese

Preheat oven to 350°. Butter a shallow baking dish.

In a large saucepan cook the spinach with just the water that clings to it until spinach wilts. Drain. Squeeze dry.

In a small saucepan melt the butter and sauté the scallions until just tender. Stir in the flour. Gradually stir in the cream.

Bring the sauce to a boil, lower heat and simmer 2 minutes, stirring constantly. Season with salt and pepper. Add the nutmeg, Worcestershire sauce and Gruyère cheese. Stir until cheese has melted.

Mix spinach with half the sauce and spread on the bottom of the baking dish. Arrange the fish fillets on top.

Pour remaining sauce over all and sprinkle with the Parmesan cheese. Bake until fish flakes easily, about 20 minutes.

6 servings

Fillets of Fish with Lemon Sauce

2 pounds fish fillets (sole,
  flounder, cod)
1 cup milk
1 1/2 cups water
1 bay leaf

4 sprigs parsley
4 whole peppercorns
1/2 teaspoon salt
2 whole cloves
Lemon Sauce

In a saucepan arrange the fish fillets in one layer. Add the milk and water until fish is barely covered. Add the bay leaf, parsley sprigs, peppercorns, salt and cloves.

Cover and simmer until fish flakes easily when tested with a fork, about 3 to 4 minutes. Reserve 1/4 cup of liquid.

Transfer to a serving platter and spoon Lemon Sauce over top.

Lemon Sauce

4 tablespoons (1/2 stick) unsalted butter
1/2 teaspoon minced garlic
3 tablespoons finely chopped shallots

juice of 1/2 lemon
1/4 cup reserved fish liquid
2 tablespoons finely minced fresh parsley
salt and pepper to taste

In a saucepan heat 1 tablespoon of the butter and sauté the garlic and shallots until softened.

Stir in the reserved fish liquid. Bring to a boil and add the lemon juice. Swirl in the remaining 3 tablespoons butter. Remove from heat and add the parsley. Adjust seasoning with salt and pepper.

4 servings

Flounder Fillets with Dill

12 flounder fillets
salt and pepper to taste
2 tablespoons finely chopped fresh dill
2 teaspoons Dijon mustard
4 tablespoons (1/2 stick) unsalted butter, melted

3 tablespoons lemon juice
1 teaspoon soy sauce
2 tablespoons fine fresh bread crumbs
2 scallions, chopped

Preheat broiler. Butter a baking dish large enough to hold four fish fillets in one layer. There will be three layers.

Sprinkle each fillet with salt and pepper and arrange four fillets, skin side down, in one layer in the dish. Divide the dill into two portions and sprinkle top of fillets with one portion of the dill.

Divide each of the following into three equal portions: mustard, melted butter, and the combined soy sauce and lemon juice. Put a third of each on top of the dill on each fillet. Cover with four more fillets and top each layer with the remaining portion of dill and a third of the other ingredients. Place the last four fillets on each stack and top each with the last third of the ingredients. Sprinkle the bread crumbs equally over the four stacks.

Broil the fish 6 inches from the heat about 5 minutes, being careful that the bread crumbs do not burn. Turn broiler to bake and lower heat to 450°. Sprinkle scallions over fish and bake 5 minutes. Remove from the oven and baste the fish with the cooking liquid before serving.

4 servings

aked Halibut

3 pounds halibut fillets
1 cup finely chopped fresh
  parsley
salt and pepper to taste
juice of 1 lemon
3 onions, thinly sliced
2 garlic cloves, minced

a 14-ounce can whole tomatoes
  with juice
1 cup white wine
1 cup clam broth
1/3 cup olive oil
4 fresh tomatoes, sliced
dried oregano to taste

Preheat oven to 350°.

Spread half of the chopped parsley on the bottom of a baking dish. Place the halibut fillets on top of the parsley. Season with salt and pepper and pour the lemon juice over the fillets.

In a bowl combine the onions, garlic, the remaining parsley, canned tomatoes, wine, clam broth and olive oil. Mix and pour over the fish.

Place the fresh tomato slices on top of the fish. Sprinkle with the oregano and bake for one hour, basting occasionally.

6 servings

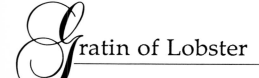ratin of Lobster

4 carrots, sliced
2 onions, sliced
1 bay leaf
1 1/2 cups dry white wine
3 cups water

three 2-pound lobsters
1/3 cup clarified butter
Lobster Sauce
salt and pepper to taste
1 teaspoon lemon juice

In a large kettle add the carrots, onion, bay leaf, wine and water. Bring to a boil, lower heat and simmer for 20 minutes. Add the lobsters and poach them until they just turn pink.

Remove meat from shells and cut into small pieces, reserving the shells. Chop 2 tablespoons lobster meat and reserve for Lobster Sauce.

In a saucepan heat the butter and sauté the lobster 5 minutes. Add the Lobster Sauce and mix carefully. Adjust seasoning with salt and pepper. Add the lemon juice. Transfer to a gratin dish and run under the broiler until top is browned.

Lobster Sauce

2 tablespoons unsalted butter
1/4 cup flour
2 cups milk
1 carrot, chopped
1 small onion stuck with 2 cloves
bouquet garni in cheesecloth bag
  (parsley, bay leaf, celery)

1 cup heavy cream
6 tablespoons Lobster Butter
2 tablespoons of the reserved
  chopped lobster
1 teaspoon tomato paste

In a saucepan melt the butter and stir in the flour, whisking continuously until smooth. Slowly add the milk while continuing to whisk, until thickened. Add the carrot, onion and bouquet garni and simmer for 10 minutes. Strain into another saucepan. Add the cream and reduce sauce by a third. Force through a sieve. Add the Lobster Butter, the reserved chopped lobster and the tomato paste.

Lobster Butter

1 1/2 cups lobster shells
8 tablespoons (1 stick) unsalted
  butter

3 tablespoons boiling water

Must be prepared in advance.

Preheat oven to 375°.

Place shells in a baking pan and set in oven for about 10 minutes. Crush the shells in a food processor. Transfer to the top of a double boiler, add the butter and cook for 10 minutes. Strain through a cheesecloth. Add the boiling water and let stand 5 minutes. Strain the water into the strained butter. Pour into a bowl, cover and refrigerate for three to four hours. Remove the butter and discard the liquid.

6 servings

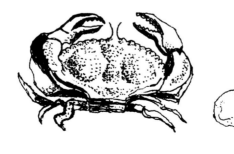

Mussels and Shrimp with Rice

3 pounds mussels
1 cup water
1 pound shrimp, peeled and
  deveined
1 tablespoon minced fresh parsley
1 cup tomato juice
  (approximately)

4 tablespoons (1/2 stick) unsalted
  butter
1 onion, finely chopped
1 clove garlic, minced
1 cup long-grain rice
salt and white pepper to taste

Scrub mussels well under cold running water.

In a large saucepan bring the water to a boil and add the mussels. Cover and steam, shaking pan occasionally until mussel shells have opened, about 5 minutes.

Remove mussels with a slotted spoon, discarding any unopened shells. Reserve the cooking liquid. Remove mussels from shells. Combine with shrimp and parsley. Set aside.

Strain the reserved liquid through several thicknesses of cheesecloth. Measure and add enough tomato juice to make 2 cups. Set aside.

In a 4-quart saucepan melt the butter. Add the onion and garlic and sauté until onion is soft. Do not let it brown. Stir in the rice. Add the mussel tomato liquid and bring to a boil. Cover, lower heat and simmer until rice is almost done, about 15 minutes.

Arrange mussels and shrimp over rice. Cover and cook until the shrimp are pink and the rice is cooked, about 7 minutes.

Before serving, stir through several times. Adjust seasoning with salt and pepper.

6 servings

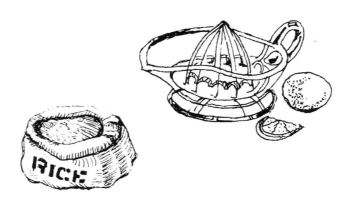

Oysters New Orleans

4 dozen (4 pints) shucked oysters, drained
8 tablespoons (1 stick) unsalted butter
1/2 cup olive oil
1/2 cup chopped onion
2 tablespoons minced garlic

1/4 cup chopped fresh parsley
1 cup seasoned bread crumbs
1/2 cup grated Parmesan cheese
salt and pepper to taste
1/2 teaspoon red pepper
3 slices bacon, cut into small pieces

Preheat oven to 350°. Spread the oysters on paper towels to dry.

In a large saucepan melt the butter with the oil and sauté the onion, garlic, and parsley until onion is soft. Do not let onion brown. Set aside.

In a bowl combine the bread crumbs, Parmesan cheese, salt and pepper and red pepper. Stir into the onion mixture. Gently fold the oysters into the bread crumb mixture. Divide among six ovenproof baking dishes. Top with the bacon. Bake, uncovered, until bacon is cooked and top is browned, about 30 minutes.

Can be made in advance and baked just before serving.

6 servings

Grilled Salmon Steaks

3 pounds salmon steaks
1/2 cup olive oil
3 tablespoons fresh lime juice
1 tablespoon Champagne mustard

3 tablespoons minced scallions
1/4 cup chopped fresh dill
salt and pepper to taste

Must be prepared in advance.

In a small bowl beat together the oil, lime juice, mustard, scallions, dill and salt and pepper.

Marinate the salmon steaks for one hour or more.

Grill or broil 7 to 8 minutes per side, brushing with the marinade.

6 servings

Broiled Scallops

2 pounds bay scallops
1/2 cup flour
1/4 cup soft bread crumbs
red pepper to taste
1/2 teaspoon paprika

salt and white pepper to taste
juice of 1 lemon
8 tablespoons (1 stick) unsalted
  butter, melted

Preheat the broiler.

In a bowl combine the flour, bread crumbs, red pepper, paprika and salt and pepper. Coat scallops lightly in the mixture and arrange them in one layer in a baking dish. Sprinkle the lemon juice over all. Pour the butter on top.

Broil until golden on one side. Turn and cook until golden on the other. Do not overcook.

4 servings

Scallops Creole

1 1/2 pounds bay scallops
3 tablespoons unsalted butter
1/2 cup chopped onion
1/2 cup chopped celery
1 clove garlic, minced
a 14-ounce can imported whole
  tomatoes with juice, crushed
an 8-ounce can tomato sauce
salt to taste

1 teaspoon sugar (optional)
1 tablespoon Worcestershire
  sauce
1/2 -1 teaspoon chili powder
dash Tabasco sauce
2 tablespoons cornstarch
1 tablespoon cold water
1/2 cup chopped green pepper

In a large saucepan melt the butter and sauté the onion, celery and garlic until tender but not browned.

In a bowl combine the tomatoes, tomato sauce, salt, sugar, Worcestershire sauce, chili powder and Tabasco sauce with the onion mixture. Simmer, uncovered, for 45 minutes.

In a small bowl mix the cornstarch with the water and stir into the sauce. Cook, stirring, until mixture thickens and begins to bubble. Add the scallops and green pepper. Cover and simmer 5 minutes longer.

4 servings

$\mathscr{S}$callops with Brandy

6 tablespoons unsalted butter
1 large onion, finely chopped
1 1/2 pounds bay scallops
1/4 cup flour seasoned with 1/4 teaspoon salt and pinch of pepper
1/2 teaspoon curry powder or to taste
pinch of red pepper

2 tablespoons brandy
1/2 cup white wine
3 tomatoes, peeled, seeded and coarsely chopped
1 tablespoon finely chopped fresh parsley
salt and white pepper to taste
3 tablespoons toasted bread crumbs

In a saucepan melt 3 tablespoons of the butter and sauté the onion until soft but not brown. Pat the scallops dry with paper towels and toss in the seasoned flour to coat lightly. Sauté the scallops over medium-high heat, stirring occasionally, 2 minutes. Sprinkle in the curry powder and red pepper. Continue cooking until golden brown, about 2 minutes.

Add the brandy and flame. Add the wine and tomatoes and simmer until the wine is well reduced and the tomatoes are very soft, about 3 minutes. Do not overcook. If there is too much liquid, remove the scallops and boil the liquid down. Add the parsley. Adjust seasoning with salt and pepper and return the scallops to the liquid. Spoon the mixture into four scallop shells.

In a small saucepan melt the remaining butter. Sprinkle the scallops with the bread crumbs and top with the butter.

Can be made a day in advance up to this point.

Before serving, heat under the broiler until very hot and browned.

4 servings

HORS D'OEUVRES AT THE PLAYHOUSE

As Westport changed from an industrial river town to a residential and artists' community, many of its architectural landmarks reflected that change. Where once the Kemper Tannery operated, there now exists the world-famous Westport Country Playhouse. Internationally known for its summer stock and original performances, the Playhouse has been a mecca for actors and actresses from Broadway, Hollywood and television for many years. The dress in this picture, for example, was specially created for Leslie Caron.

$\mathcal{S}$hrimp Provençal

1 1/2 pounds shrimp, peeled and
   deveined
2 teaspoons olive oil
1 onion, minced
1 clove garlic, minced
1/2 cup dry white wine
a 14-ounce can tomatoes with
   juice, crushed

1 tablespoon minced fresh parsley
   plus 1 teaspoon for garnish
1/2 teaspoon dried oregano
salt and pepper to taste
4 tablespoons grated Parmesan
   cheese

In a saucepan heat the olive oil and sauté the onion and garlic. Add 1 tablespoon white wine and cook, stirring just until wine evaporates and onion begins to brown. Stir in the tomatoes, parsley, oregano, the remaining wine and salt and pepper. Simmer, uncovered, for 5 minutes.

Arrange shrimp on top of tomato mixture and continue to simmer until shrimp is pink and cooked through, 3 to 5 minutes longer. Sprinkle with Parmesan cheese and parsley.

4 servings

$\mathcal{B}$arbecued Shrimp

1 pound large shrimp
1/3 cup vegetable oil
1/3 cup sherry
1/3 cup soy sauce
1 clove garlic, crushed

2 bay leaves
2 teaspoons Worcestershire sauce
dash Tabasco sauce
Butter Sauce

Must be prepared a day in advance.

Rinse shrimp leaving shells on.

In a bowl combine the oil, sherry, soy sauce, garlic, bay leaves, Worcestershire sauce and Tabasco sauce. Add the shrimp and marinate in the refrigerator overnight, turning occasionally.

Prepare grill and barbecue shrimp about 5 minutes, being careful not to overcook.

Serve with Butter Sauce.

Butter Sauce
juice of 1 lemon
8 tablespoons (1 stick) unsalted
   butter, melted

2 teaspoons soy sauce or to taste

Combine all the ingredients.

4 servings

$\mathscr{S}$hrimp Rémoulade

2 pounds shrimp in the shell
1 bay leaf
1 small onion
1 clove garlic, crushed
6 black peppercorns, crushed
6 white peppercorns, crushed

1/4 teaspoon dried thyme
Rémoulade Sauce
lettuce leaves, thinly sliced
 shredded lettuce, lemon and
 tomato wedges

Put unshelled shrimp in a saucepan and add water to cover. Add the seasonings and bring to a boil. Lower heat and simmer, uncovered, until shrimp are cooked, about 3 minutes. Drain and refrigerate the shrimp. When cool, peel and devein shrimp and return to the refrigerator until well chilled.

In a bowl combine the shrimp and Rémoulade Sauce. Place lettuce leaves on four plates and mound about 1/3 cup shredded lettuce in the center. Divide shrimp and arrange on top of lettuce. Garnish with lemon and tomato wedges.

Rémoulade Sauce
2 egg yolks
1/4 cup vegetable oil
1/4 cup finely chopped celery
1/2 cup chopped fresh parsley
1/2 cup finely chopped scallions
1/4 cup grated horseradish,
 preferably fresh
2 tablespoons lemon juice
2 tablespoons Creole mustard
1 tablespoon brown mustard

2 tablespoons ketchup
2 tablespoons Worcestershire
 sauce
3 cloves garlic, minced
1 tablespoon tarragon wine
 vinegar
2 teaspoons paprika
salt and pepper to taste
Tabasco sauce to taste

Must be prepared a day in advance.

In a food processor beat the egg yolks 2 minutes. With the machine running add the oil in a steady stream. Add the remaining ingredients, one at a time, until well mixed. Transfer to a bowl, cover and refrigerate.

4 servings

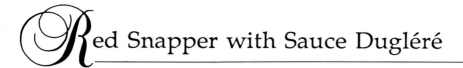ed Snapper with Sauce Dugléré

Contributed by Owner-Chef, George Llorens,
Dameon's, Westport

4 tablespoons (1/2 stick) unsalted butter, melted	4 tablespoons finely chopped shallots
4 red snapper fillets	salt and white pepper to taste
1 cup white wine	Sauce Dugléré

Must be prepared a day in advance.

In an overproof baking dish place the red snapper fillets on top of the butter. Add the wine, shallots and salt and pepper. Cover and marinate overnight in the refrigerator.

Preheat oven to 400°.

Let the fillets come to room temperature. Set the baking dish in the oven and poach the fillets for 8 to 10 minutes.

Remove the red snapper with a slotted spoon to a heated serving platter. Transfer the marinade to a small saucepan and prepare Sauce Dugléré.

Sauce Dugléré

4 tablespoons (1/2 stick) unsalted butter	4 fresh basil leaves
1/2 cup heavy cream	1/4 teaspoon sugar
3 tomatoes, peeled, cored and chopped	1/4 cup chopped chives

In the saucepan with the marinade add the butter and the cream. Bring to a boil and reduce the liquid by half. Add the tomatoes, basil leaves and sugar and cook for 5 minutes. Stir in the chives.

Before serving, remove basil leaves.

4 servings

illets of Sole with Mushrooms

1 1/2 pounds fillets of sole	salt and pepper to taste
4 tablespoons (1/2 stick) unsalted butter	1/4 cup dry white wine
	1/2 cup light cream
1 medium onion, finely chopped	1 tablespoon flour
1/4 pound fresh mushrooms, thinly sliced	paprika and finely chopped fresh parsley for garnish
1/4 cup chopped fresh parsley	

Preheat oven to 350°. Butter a baking dish.

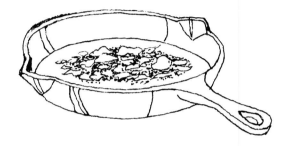

In a saucepan melt 3 tablespoons of the butter and sauté the onion and mushrooms until softened. Stir in the parsley.

Place the fillets in a single layer in the prepared baking dish. Sprinkle with salt and pepper. Cover with the mushroom mixture. Pour white wine over fillets and top with remaining butter.

Bake for 15 minutes. Remove from oven and drain fish liquid into a small saucepan.

In a small bowl combine the cream and flour. Add to the fish liquid and blend well. Cook, stirring constantly until thickened. Pour over fillets. Sprinkle with paprika and parsley. Bake an additional 5 minutes or until fish flakes easily.

4 servings

Broiled Swordfish Steak with Rosemary

a 2-pound swordfish steak, cut
  into 4 pieces
3 tablespoons olive oil
juice of 1 lemon
1/2 teaspoon dried thyme

kosher salt and pepper to taste
2 shallots, coarsely chopped
4 ripe tomatoes, peeled, skinned
  and chopped
1 teaspoon dried rosemary

Must be prepared in advance.

In a bowl combine 2 tablespoons of the oil with the lemon juice, thyme, salt and pepper. Brush the mixture on the swordfish and marinate one hour.

In a saucepan heat the remaining 1 tablespoon oil and sauté the shallots. Add the tomatoes and rosemary and cook for 3 to 4 minutes, stirring occasionally. Set aside.

Broil the swordfish for 5 to 7 minutes, turn and broil for about 3 minutes longer. Transfer to a serving dish and place the tomato rosemary mixture on the side.

4 servings

Trout Baked in Wine

6 trout, cleaned
salt
1/2 cup plus 3 tablespoons fresh
  bread crumbs
1/4 teaspoon nutmeg
1/4 teaspoon pepper

1/2 teaspoon dried thyme
2 teaspoons chopped fresh
  parsley
1/2 cup dry white wine
4 tablespoons (1/2 stick) unsalted
  butter, melted

Preheat oven to 350°. Butter a shallow baking dish.

Score one side of each trout with diagonal slashes just through the skin, about one inch apart. Season with salt.

In a bowl combine the 1/2 cup bread crumbs with the nutmeg, pepper, thyme and parsley. Spread half the mixture over the bottom of the dish. Arrange trout in a single layer on top of the crumbs. Pour wine over all. Brush trout with the butter. Sprinkle with remaining bread crumbs.

Bake, basting often, until fish flakes easily, about 20 to 25 minutes.

6 servings

hicken Stuffed with Veal

Contributed by Chef Robert Pouget, Le Chambord, Westport

two 2 1/2-pound whole chickens
1/2 pound ground veal
3 slices white bread soaked in
   1 cup heavy cream
salt and pepper to taste
2 shallots, finely minced

3 ounces chanterelles, coarsely
   chopped
2 teaspoons minced fresh parsley
Mushroom Sauce
Chicken Stock

Preheat oven to 375°.

Bone the chickens, keeping only leg bones in place. Cut the chickens in half, lengthwise. Reserve the chicken bones.

In a bowl mix together the remaining ingredients until well blended. Divide the mixture into 4 portions and stuff each chicken thigh. Fold the breast over to create a pear shape. Place in a roasting pan and bake one hour.

Serve with Mushroom Sauce.

Mushroom Sauce
1 teaspoon unsalted butter
1 teaspoon flour
1/2 cup heavy cream

1/4 cup white mushrooms,
   coarsely chopped
Chicken Stock

In a saucepan melt the butter and blend in the flour, whisking until it becomes foamy. Do not let it brown. Remove from heat, pour in 2 cups of simmering Chicken Stock. Blend vigorously. Slowly pour in the heavy cream and add the mushrooms.

Chicken Stock
the chicken bones
1 stalk celery, coarsely chopped
1 carrot, coarsely chopped
1 onion

2 sprigs parsley
dash of thyme
1 bay leaf
1 cup white wine

Cover the chicken bones with water. Add the remaining ingredients and simmer, uncovered, for 1 hour.

4 servings

Chicken with Orange Peel

2 whole chicken breasts, boned,
  skinned and cut into bite-size
  pieces
peel of 1 large, thick-skinned
  orange
1 egg yolk, beaten
2 tablespoons cornstarch
1 tablespoon vegetable oil
1 tablespoon soy sauce

2 teaspoons sugar
1/4 cup vegetable oil
1 teaspoon finely chopped fresh
  ginger
5 -10 dry, whole chili peppers
2 scallions, chopped
1 clove garlic, chopped
dash of sesame oil
Chinese vinegar to taste

Must be prepared in advance.

Cut orange peel into small pieces. Set aside and allow to dry, uncovered, at least one hour and preferably overnight.

In a bowl combine the egg, cornstarch and oil. Add the chicken and stir to coat. Marinate for about one hour.

In a small bowl mix the soy sauce and sugar and set aside.

Place 1/4 cup oil in preheated wok. Add the orange peel and stir fry until the peel just starts to brown. Remove peel and set aside.

Add the chicken, ginger, chili peppers, scallions and garlic and stir fry until cooked. Add the soy sauce mixture and the reserved orange peel. Mix thoroughly.

Just before serving, add the sesame oil and vinegar.

4 servings

uttermilk Pecan Chicken

6 pounds chicken breasts, halved
1/3 cup chopped pecans
2 tablespoons sesame seeds
1 teaspoon paprika
1 teaspoon salt
pepper to taste

1 cup flour
1 egg yolk, beaten
1/2 cup buttermilk
6 tablespoons unsalted butter,
  melted
2 tablespoons whole pecans

Preheat oven to 350°.

In a bowl mix together the chopped pecans, sesame seeds, paprika, salt, pepper and flour.
In another bowl beat together the egg yolk and buttermilk.
Dip the chicken in the egg mixture and coat with the seasoned flour.
Pour the butter into the roasting pan, add the chicken and turn to coat. Bake 30 minutes.
Sprinkle chicken with whole pecans and bake until chicken is tender, about 30 minutes longer.

8 servings

arbecued Chicken

6 chicken breasts, halved
3 tablespoons Dijon mustard
1 cup safflower oil
2 cloves garlic, crushed
1 1/2 teaspoons crushed dried
  thyme

1 large bay leaf, crumbled
pinch red pepper
2 1/2 tablespoons white wine
2 1/2 tablespoons vinegar
salt to taste

Must be prepared a day in advance.

In a small bowl combine the mustard with the oil. Mix in the remaining ingredients. Pour marinade over chicken breasts, cover and refrigerate overnight, turning occasionally.
Barbecue chicken breasts 8 to 10 minutes on each side, basting frequently with the marinade.

6 to 8 servings

hicken Tarragon

3 whole chicken breasts, skinned
   and halved + boneal?
salt and pepper to taste
1/4 cup flour
4 tablespoons (1/2 stick) unsalted
   butter

1 tablespoon chopped shallot
1/4 cup white Bordeaux wine
1/2 teaspoon dried tarragon
3/4 cup chicken broth
1/4 cup heavy cream

Sprinkle the chicken breasts with salt and pepper and coat with the flour. Reserve the flour.

In a large saucepan melt 3 tablespoons of the butter, add the chicken and brown on all sides. Remove

Add the shallot to the pan and sauté briefly. Add the wine and cook over high heat until the liquids are nearly evaporated while scraping loose all browned particles. Remove chicken .

Add the reserved flour and stir with a whisk to make a thick paste. Sprinkle in the tarragon and stir in the broth.

* Return the chicken to the saucepan, cover and cook until tender, about 25 minutes. Transfer the chicken to a platter. In the same saucepan add the remaining butter and cream and heat, Heat, stirring continuously. Pour sauce over chicken. Broth .

* If boneless, cook 6 min.
add more broth, if necc. to sauce + no cream

(6 servings)

153

Chicken in Cream Sauce

4 whole chicken breasts, skinned,
  boned and halved
1 cup flour
salt and white pepper to taste
6 tablespoons (3/4 stick) unsalted
  butter
1 teaspoon vegetable oil
1/2-3/4 cup chicken broth
1 T sherry

1 cup heavy cream
juice of 1 lemon
8 large mushrooms, stemmed and
  sliced
1/2 cup cooked peas
2 tablespoons flour
chopped fresh parsley or dill for
  garnish

Season flour with salt and pepper and coat chicken breasts.

In a large saucepan melt 2 tablespoons of the butter with the oil and sauté chicken over high heat until browned on all sides. Add 1/2 cup chicken broth and bring to a boil. Lower heat, cover and simmer 6 minutes, adding more broth if necessary. Remove chicken and stir in the cream and lemon juice. Cook until liquids are reduced by half. Return chicken to saucepan and keep warm.

In another saucepan melt another 2 tablespoons butter. Add the mushrooms and sauté until lightly browned. Combine the mushrooms and peas with the chicken. Bring almost to a boil.

With the fingertips knead together the remaining butter and flour. Stir in just enough to thicken sauce slightly. Adjust seasoning with salt and pepper. Transfer to a serving platter and sprinkle with the parsley or dill.

4 to 6 servings

Curried Chicken

2 1/2 pounds cooked chicken
  breasts, cut into bite size pieces
6 tablespoons unsalted butter
1 cup minced onion
1 cup chopped celery
4 cloves garlic, minced
1/2 cup flour
1-2 tablespoons curry powder

1 teaspoon dry mustard
1/2 teaspoon salt
1/4 teaspoon pepper
1 teaspoon paprika
dash of red pepper
1 1/4 cups beef broth
1 cup light cream
3 tablespoons ketchup

Prepare a day in advance to allow the flavors to blend.

In a saucepan melt the butter and sauté the onion, celery and garlic until onion is softened. Combine all of the dry ingredients and add to the onion mixture, stirring with a whisk until well blended. Slowly add the beef broth and cream and stir until smooth. Mix in the ketchup. Cook for 2 minutes. Add the chicken and heat thoroughly.

6 servings

$\mathcal{H}$erb Roasted Chicken

two 3-pound chickens	1 teaspoon dried thyme
1/2 cup olive oil	3 teaspoons red wine vinegar
1/2 cup corn oil	2 cups chicken broth
6 cloves garlic, finely chopped	salt and pepper to taste
1 teaspoon dried rosemary	2 tablespoons unsalted butter

Must be prepared a day in advance.

In a large bowl combine the olive oil, corn oil, garlic, rosemary and 1/2 teaspoon of the thyme. Place chickens in the marinade, cover and refrigerate, turning occasionally, overnight.

Preheat oven to 375°.

Scrape the herbs from the chickens and place in a roasting pan. Cook the chickens until nicely browned, about 45 minutes.

Remove the chickens from the roasting pan and pour off all but 2 tablespoons of the fat. Add the vinegar, broth, the remaining 1/2 teaspoon thyme, and salt and pepper to taste. Bring to a boil and cook about 3 minutes. Stir in the butter.

Carve the chickens and arrange on a serving platter. Spoon the sauce on top.

6 to 8 servings

Baked Chicken with Artichokes and Mushrooms

4 whole chicken breasts, boned,
 skinned and halved
salt and pepper to taste
1 teaspoon paprika
6 tablespoons oil
a 14-ounce can artichoke hearts,
 drained

2 tablespoons lemon juice
1 pound mushrooms, sliced
1 clove garlic, chopped
3 tablespoons flour
1 cup chicken broth
1/4 cup sherry
1/2 teaspoon dried rosemary

Preheat oven to 350°.

Season chicken breasts with salt, pepper and paprika.

In a large saucepan heat the oil and sauté the chicken breasts. Transfer to a shallow baking dish. In the same saucepan sauté the artichoke hearts until they are browned. Arrange the artichoke hearts around the chicken and sprinkle with the lemon juice.

In the same saucepan sauté the mushrooms and garlic for 8 minutes. Pour off any pan juices that remain in the saucepan. Sprinkle flour over mushrooms and stir well. Add chicken broth, stirring to pick up any browned particles that remain in the saucepan.

Add the sherry and rosemary. Cook over low heat for 5 minutes, stirring with a whisk until the sauce is smooth and thick. Pour sauce over chicken. *Can be made in advance. Refrigerate until ready to bake.*

Bake for 35 to 40 minutes.

4 to 6 servings

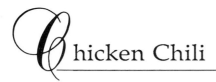# hicken Chili

6 whole chicken breasts, boned and halved	1 large onion, finely chopped
3 eggs, lightly beaten	3 cloves garlic, minced
1 1/2 cups seasoned bread crumbs	2/3 cup (6 ounces) chopped, canned mild green chilies
2/3 cup plus 2 tablespoons vegetable oil	a 14-ounce can tomatoes with juice, crushed
6 tablespoons unsalted butter	an 8-ounce package cream cheese, softened
1 large green pepper, finely chopped	1 1/2 to 2 cups buttermilk

Preheat oven to 325°.

Pound the chicken breasts with the flat side of a knife to shape into cutlets.

Dip the chicken in the egg and coat lightly with the bread crumbs. Set cutlets on a wire rack to dry for 15 minutes.

In a saucepan heat the 2/3 cup oil with the butter and sauté the chicken until lightly browned on both sides. Set aside.

In another saucepan heat the 2 tablespoons oil and sauté the green pepper, onion and garlic until tender. Add the chilies and the tomatoes. Stir in the cream cheese and combine to make a creamy sauce.

In a 3-quart oval baking dish, spoon a third of the sauce over the bottom. Layer 5 or 6 of the cutlets, cover with half of the remaining sauce and add the remaining cutlets. Cover with the rest of the sauce.

Pour the buttermilk over the chicken, barely covering it. Shake the baking dish to distribute the buttermilk.

Bake for 30 minutes, uncovered, until bubbly.

Can be baked the day before and reheated at 325° for about 30 minutes. If it looks dry, add more buttermilk.

6 to 8 servings

Chicken in Wine Sauce

a 3 1/2-pound chicken, cut into
  serving pieces
flour for coating
salt and pepper to taste
1/4 -1/2 cup olive oil
2 tablespoons unsalted butter

2 cloves garlic, minced
1/2 cup dry white wine
juice of 1 lemon
3 tablespoons finely chopped
  fresh parsley

Season the flour with salt and pepper and coat the chicken.

In a heavy saucepan large enough to hold the chicken pieces in one layer, heat the oil and add the chicken, skin side down. Cook, uncovered, until golden brown, 8 to 10 minutes on each side.

Remove chicken and pour all the fat from the saucepan. Return the chicken to the saucepan and add the butter and garlic. Pour the wine around the chicken and bring to a boil. Pour the lemon juice over the chicken and sprinkle with the parsley. Cover and cook 3 minutes longer.

4 servings

Chicken with Mushrooms

a 3 1/2-pound broiler chicken, cut
  into serving pieces
4 strips bacon, cut into small
  pieces
2 tablespoons chopped onion
2 tablespoons cognac
8 small whole onions, peeled
1 carrot, coarsely chopped
1 clove garlic, crushed

2 cups Burgundy wine
2 tablespoons unsalted butter
1 pound mushrooms, sliced
a bouquet garni tied in
  cheesecloth bag (4 sprigs
  parsley, 1 bay leaf, 1/4
  teaspoon dried thyme, 3 sprigs
  celery leaves)

Preheat oven to 350°.

In a saucepan cook the bacon and the chopped onion until the bacon is cooked. Remove with a slotted spoon.

Brown the chicken in the bacon drippings and transfer to a platter.

In the same saucepan add the cognac, onions, carrot and garlic and cook until tender, about 4 minutes. Remove vegetables and set aside. Add the wine and bring to a boil, stirring to loosen the browned particles in the bottom of the saucepan.

Meanwhile, in another saucepan melt the butter and sauté the mushrooms until lightly browned.

Place the bouquet garni in the bottom of a 3-quart baking dish and arrange the chicken, bacon, vegetables and mushrooms in layers. Pour the wine over all. Bake, covered, for 1 1/2 hours.

4 servings

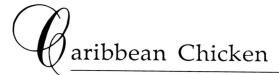aribbean Chicken

a 3 1/2-pound frying chicken, cut into serving pieces
juice of 1 lemon
4 cloves garlic, minced
3 tablespoons paprika
2 tablespoons pepper
1 teaspoon salt

1/4 cup soy sauce
3 tablespoons Tabasco sauce
flour for coating
vegetable oil for frying
4 tablespoons (1/2 stick) unsalted butter

In a bowl pour the lemon juice over the chicken pieces and marinate for 1/2 hour.

In a small bowl combine the garlic, paprika, pepper, salt, soy sauce and Tabasco sauce and toss with the chicken. Marinate chicken for another 1/2 hour.

Coat the chicken with the flour.

In a heavy saucepan heat the oil with the butter, add the chicken, cover and fry until golden brown, about 20 minutes.

4 to 6 servings

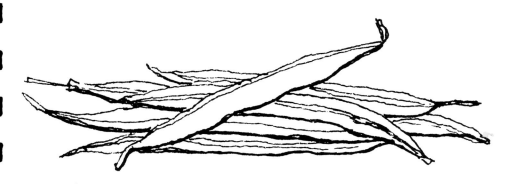

A PICNIC AT COMPO BEACH

Compo Beach is the scene of countless year-round activities in Westport, and none more favored than a picnic. This picnic scene, however, features no ordinary tablecloth. The quilt in this photograph was designed and sewn by League members to be raffled at the annual Creative Arts Festival sponsored by the League. While all League members take pride in the quilt each year, there is always a twinge of regret at seeing it raffled off. This quilt did remain in the family, since it was won by a League member.

The Creative Arts Festival, a major fundraiser for the League invites over 100 craftspeople to display their creative and original work. Thousands of people look forward to this spectacular event held each year in the fall.

The League also sponsors a five-mile road race along a scenic route in town, including the Compo Beach area. Westport's famous Minute Man Road Race, named appropriately for our Revolutionary War heroes, has become a fixture every May as runners come from many surrounding areas to compete and enjoy the view.

Chicken in Tomato Sauce

1/2 cup flour
1 teaspoon salt
1/8 teaspoon pepper
8 chicken breasts, halved = 16 halves
1/4 cup butter
1/4 cup olive oil
2 medium onions, sliced
2 cloves garlic, minced
1 green pepper, sliced
1 pound mushrooms, sliced
2 chicken bouillon cubes

a 28-ounce can Italian plum
  tomatoes, drained and
  chopped, reserving juice
2 tablespoons chopped fresh
  parsley
salt and pepper to taste
1/2 teaspoon dried oregano
1/2 teaspoon dried marjoram
1/2 teaspoon dried thyme
1/2 cup dry white wine
opt. {1/2 cup sliced ripe olives
  grated Parmesan cheese

Preheat oven to 350°.

Season the flour with salt and pepper and coat the chicken breasts.

In a large saucepan heat the butter and oil and brown the chicken. Remove with a slotted spoon to a 9x13-inch baking pan. In the same saucepan sauté the onion, garlic, green pepper and mushrooms. Stir in the bouillon cubes, tomatoes, parsley, salt and pepper, oregano, marjoram and thyme, white wine and 1/2 cup of the reserved tomato juice. Cook 5 minutes.

Pour sauce over chicken, cover and bake until chicken is almost *less if boned* tender, about 45 minutes. Remove cover, add olives and bake 15 to 20 minutes longer. Transfer chicken and vegetables to a platter and rapidly boil pan liquids until slightly reduced and thickened. Pour over chicken. Sprinkle with Parmesan cheese.

25 min covered
5 min - uncovered

8 servings

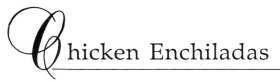

Chicken Enchiladas

3 tablespoons unsalted butter
1 onion, thinly sliced
3/4 cup cooked chicken (about 1 large breast), shredded
2 tablespoons green chilies or to taste
a 3-ounce package cream cheese, softened and cut into pieces
salt to taste

oil for frying
4 flour tortillas
1/3 cup whipping cream
1 cup grated Monterey Jack cheese
chopped scallions, sliced black olives and lime wedges for garnish
lime juice to taste

Preheat oven to 375°. Butter a 9x13-inch baking dish.

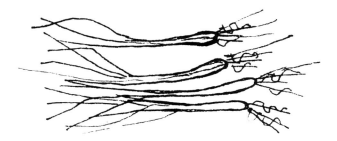

In a large saucepan melt the butter and sauté the onion until it is soft, about 20 minutes. Remove from heat and add the chicken, chilies and cream cheese. Mix lightly with a fork. Add salt to taste.

In another saucepan heat 2 tablespoons of oil. Fry the tortillas, one at a time, for several seconds until they begin to blister and soften. Do not let them become crisp. Remove and drain on paper towels.

Spoon about 1/3 cup of filling down center of each tortilla. Roll and place seam side down in baking dish. Moisten tops with the cream and sprinkle with the Monterey Jack cheese.

Bake, uncovered, until heated through, about 20 minutes.

Garnish with scallions, olives and lime wedges. Before serving, squeeze lime juice over the top.

4 to 6 servings

163

Jack Daniels Smoked Turkey

1 frozen turkey (about 13 pounds)
brine made with 1/2 pound salt
  per gallon of water
1 cup sugar
a 4-ounce bottle liquid smoke

1 bay leaf
1 tablespoon Worcestershire
  sauce
Whiskey Sauce

Must be prepared 36 hours in advance.

In a saucepan heat the brine with the sugar until the salt and sugar are dissolved. Place the frozen turkey *(do not defrost)* in a large crock or pot (a clean bucket is perfect). Cover the turkey with the brine. Add 2 ounces of the liquid smoke, the bay leaf and Worcestershire sauce. Soak 36 hours in a cool place. *Do not refrigerate.*

Drain, pat dry, rub skin with remaining 2 ounces of liquid smoke and roast the turkey according to package directions, basting every 15 to 20 minutes with Whiskey Sauce.

Whiskey Sauce
1 pound (4 sticks) unsalted butter   1/2 cup Jack Daniels whiskey

In a small saucepan melt the butter and stir in the Jack Daniels.

12 servings

Barbecued Cornish Hens

4 cornish hens, split in half

Barbecue the cornish hens 10 to 15 minutes per side, basting often with Chili Paprika Basting Sauce.

Chili Paprika Basting Sauce
2 tablespoons peanut oil
3/4 cup cider vinegar
1 teaspoon finely minced garlic
1/2 teaspoon sugar
1 tablespoon chili powder

1 teaspoon dry mustard
1 teaspoon paprika
1/2 teaspoon ground cumin
salt and pepper to taste

In a small bowl combine all the ingredients and mix well.

4 to 8 servings

Cornish Hens with Cornbread Apple Stuffing

three 2 1/2-pound cornish hens
salt and pepper to taste
paprika to taste

Cornbread Apple Stuffing
Basting Sauce

Preheat oven to 350°.

Fill the cornish hens with the Cornbread Apple Stuffing and truss the hens. Rub the skins with a mixture of salt, pepper and paprika.

Place in a roasting pan and cook for 1 hour, basting frequently with the Basting Sauce and pan juices.

Cornbread Apple Stuffing

1 medium onion, coarsely chopped
3 apples, peeled and sliced
4 tablespoons (1/2 stick) unsalted
   butter

3 cups crumbled cornbread
1/3 cup currants

In a saucepan melt the butter and sauté the onion and apples. Toss lightly with the cornbread and add the currants.

Basting Sauce

1 cup (2 sticks) unsalted butter,
   melted
1 tablespoon paprika

1 tablespoon dried tarragon
salt and pepper to taste

In a saucepan combine all the ingredients, bring to a boil and keep warm.

6 to 8 servings

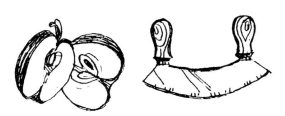

Duck with Apple Brandy

Contributed by Chef Robert Pouget, Le Chambord, Westport

2 ducklings	1 quart water
salt and pepper to taste	1 cup apple brandy
3 tablespoons unsalted butter	1 cup apple cider vinegar
2 stalks celery, chopped	5 tablespoons unsalted butter
1 large onion, chopped	2 tart green apples, peeled, cored
2 carrots, chopped	and cut in half for garnish
1 quart apple cider	dash of sugar

Must be prepared a day in advance.

Carve the duck breasts, season lightly with salt and pepper, cover and refrigerate. Reserve the legs for another use.

In a large saucepan melt 3 tablespoons of the butter and sauté the duck carcasses with the celery, onion and carrots, stirring frequently, until golden brown. Add the apple cider, water and all but 1/8 cup of the apple brandy. Bring to a boil, lower heat and simmer for 6 hours. Strain broth through a cheesecloth and remove all traces of fat.

In a small saucepan reduce the cider vinegar to half. Add to the broth and reduce the stock to 1 cup by boiling rapidly.

Place apples on a buttered baking pan. Sprinkle with apple brandy and a dash of sugar. Bake in 350° oven until cooked but still firm, about 8 minutes.

In a saucepan melt 3 tablespoons of the butter and sauté the duck breasts until cooked but still pink inside.

Before serving, heat the sauce. Remove from the heat and beat in the remaining 2 tablespoons of butter.

Pour the sauce on each serving plate. Slice the duck breast and arrange on top of the sauce. Garnish with the apples.

4 servings

Meat

*S*tuffed Fillet of Beef

1 1/2-pound beef fillet (1 1/2 inches thick)
1/2 cup dry bread crumbs
1/4 cup minced cooked bacon
1 teaspoon capers
1/2 teaspoon chopped fresh parsley
2 medium onions, finely chopped
4 tablespoons (1/2 stick) unsalted butter

2 large carrots, chopped
1 large parsnip, chopped
1 celery stalk, chopped
1/2 teaspoon flour
1/2 cup whipping cream
1/2 teaspoon paprika
salt and pepper to taste
1/4 cup Madeira wine

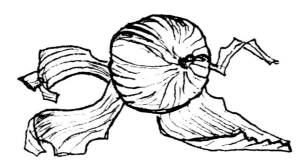

Cut a deep horizontal pocket in the beef fillet.

In a large bowl combine the bread crumbs, bacon, capers, parsley and half of the onion. Fill the fillet with the onion mixture and tie with string. Set aside.

In a large saucepan melt 2 tablespoons of the butter over medium high heat. Add the fillet and brown on both sides. Transfer to a deep saucepan. Reserve drippings.

In another saucepan melt the remaining 2 tablespoons butter. Add the remaining onion, carrots, parsnip and celery and sauté 2 to 3 minutes. Push vegetables to the side and mix in the flour and reserved drippings. Gradually stir in the cream, mixing until smooth. Combine with the vegetables from the side of the saucepan. Add the paprika and season with salt and pepper.

Pour sauce over fillet. Cover and simmer until tender, basting occasionally, about 30 minutes. Stir in the Madeira and cook 5 minutes longer.

4 to 6 servings

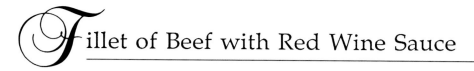illet of Beef with Red Wine Sauce

1 whole beef tenderloin
salt and pepper to taste

Red Wine Sauce

Preheat oven to 425°.

Lightly salt and pepper the fillet. Place the beef in a roasting pan and cook for about 40 minutes. After 30 minutes of cooking time, insert a meat thermometer to check degree of doneness. Meat should be cooked rare, 120°. Serve with Red Wine Sauce.

Red Wine Sauce
2 carrots, coarsely chopped
2 stalks celery, chopped
1/4 cup chopped shallots
1/2 teaspoon dried thyme
salt and pepper to taste

2 cups red Bordeaux wine
1 cup beef broth
2 tablespoons unsalted butter
1 tablespoon flour

In a saucepan combine the carrots, celery, shallots, thyme, salt, pepper and wine. Bring to a boil, lower heat and simmer, uncovered, for 10 minutes. Add the broth and cook 25 minutes longer. Strain the liquid.

With the fingertips, knead together 1 tablespoon of the butter and flour to make beurre manié. Stir into the broth a little at a time until well combined. Stir in the remaining butter. Correct seasoning with salt and pepper.

4 servings

eef Satay

1 cup water
3/4 cup finely chopped peanuts
1/2 cup soy sauce
1/4 cup lime juice
1 tablespoon unsulphured
  molasses
1/2 teaspoon minced fresh ginger

1/2 teaspoon crushed red pepper
  flakes
2 garlic cloves, minced
2 tablespoons peanut oil
1 1/2 pounds sirloin cut into 1-inch
  thick cubes
wooden skewers, soaked in cold
  water

Must be prepared in advance.

In a saucepan combine the water, peanuts, soy sauce, lime juice, molasses, ginger, red pepper and garlic. Bring to a boil, stirring often. Lower the heat and simmer, still stirring, for about 15 minutes. Let the marinade cool. Mix in the oil.

Marinate the meat in the mixture, turning occasionally, for one hour.

Thread the beef cubes on the skewers.

Grill over charcoal or broil in the oven, brushing the meat with the marinade until done, about 4 minutes on each side or to taste.

Reheat remaining marinade and serve separately as a dipping sauce.

6 servings

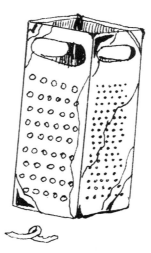

Pepper Steak with Brandy Sauce

4 filet mignons, each 1 1/4-inch or
 thicker
4 tablespoons peppercorns,
 coarsely ground
2 tablespoons unsalted butter
1 tablespoon oil

4 tablespoons brandy
4 tablespoons dry red wine
1/3 cup beef broth
4 tablespoons heavy cream, room
 temperature

Dry the steaks on paper towels. Rub and press the peppercorns into both sides of the meat.

Heat a skillet over medium high heat and melt the butter with the oil. Quickly sear the fillets on both sides to seal in the juices. Lower heat to medium and cook to desired doneness, turning often. Remove to a warm serving platter.

Pour off all but 1 tablespoon of fat. Raise the heat to high. Add brandy and wine and boil rapidly for 1 or 2 minutes to evaporate the alcohol. Add the broth and continue cooking while scraping up the browned particles in the skillet. Lower heat and slowly add the cream in a steady stream. Cook until sauce is thick and smooth. Pour the sauce over the steaks.

4 servings

eef in Tomato Sauce

3 1/2 pounds boneless chuck, cut
 into serving pieces
juice of 1 lemon
5 tablespoons olive oil
2 bay leaves
2 large onions, coarsely chopped

an 8-ounce can tomato sauce
a 13 3/4-ounce can beef broth
2 large carrots, coarsely chopped
2 stalks celery, coarsely chopped
water or broth
salt and pepper to taste

Sprinkle half the lemon juice on the meat and toss to coat. Let stand for 15 minutes.

In a heavy saucepan heat the oil and sauté the meat over high heat. Add the bay leaves and onion and continue cooking until the meat and onions are browned. Add the remaining lemon juice, the tomato sauce, broth, carrots and celery. Cook over medium low heat, uncovered and stirring frequently until meat is tender, about 2 hours, adding water or more broth, if necessary. Adjust seasoning with salt and pepper.

6 servings

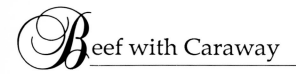

Beef with Caraway

3 pounds beef chuck, trimmed and
  cut into 2-inch cubes
5 tablespoons flour
2 teaspoons salt
1/2 teaspoon pepper
1/2 teaspoon garlic powder
4 tablespoons (1/2 stick) unsalted butter

2 cloves garlic, crushed
2 onions, chopped
1 1/2 cups apple cider
1 tablespoon tomato paste
1/2 teaspoon thyme
1 teaspoon caraway seeds
10 small whole onions

In a bowl season the flour with the salt, pepper and garlic powder and coat the meat cubes.

In a saucepan melt 2 tablespoons of the butter and sauté the garlic and onion until onion is golden. Remove with a slotted spoon. Add the remaining 2 tablespoons of butter and sear the meat on all sides. Return the onion mixture to the saucepan and add the apple cider and tomato paste. Cover and cook 2 1/2 hours.

Add the thyme, caraway seeds and whole onions. Cover and simmer until the onions are cooked and the meat is tender, about 30 minutes more.

4 to 6 servings

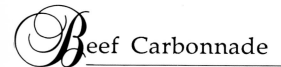

Beef Carbonnade

2 tablespoons unsalted butter
2 tablespoons olive oil
3 pounds beef chuck, cut into
  1-inch pieces
1 1/2 pounds onion, thinly sliced
salt and pepper to taste
1/8 teaspoon ground cloves
1 bottle beer

1 cup beef broth
1 tablespoon brown sugar
bouquet garni in a cheesecloth bag
  (parsley, 1/2 teaspoon thyme,
  bay leaf)
2 tablespoons cornstarch
2 tablespoons wine vinegar

In a saucepan melt the butter with the oil and brown the meat on all sides. Remove the meat with a slotted spoon. Add the onion and sauté until lightly browned. Add the garlic and cook briefly.

In an ovenproof baking dish layer the beef and onion. Pour in the beer and broth. Stir in the sugar and place the bouquet garni in the center of the dish. Cover and cook until the meat is tender, about 2 1/2 hours. Discard the bouquet garni. Mix the cornstarch with the vinegar and stir into the gravy to thicken.

6 to 8 servings

eef with Green Beans

3 pounds stewing beef, cut into 2-
  inch cubes
1 cup red Bordeaux wine
2 cloves garlic, minced
1/2 teaspoon black pepper
1 bay leaf
1/2 teaspoon thyme
2 tablespoons chopped fresh
  parsley

2 whole cloves
3 tablespoons olive oil
2 cups beef broth
10 small white onions
2 carrots, sliced
1 pound fresh green beans,
  trimmed
salt and pepper to taste

Must be prepared in advance.

In a bowl combine the wine, garlic, pepper, bay leaf, thyme, parsley, cloves and 1 tablespoon of the oil. Add the meat, cover and marinate 2 to 3 hours or overnight, turning occasionally. Drain and dry the meat with paper towels. Reserve the liquid.

In a saucepan heat the remaining oil and sauté the meat until browned on all sides. Transfer to a baking pan. Stir in the reserved marinade and enough broth so that the meat is barely covered. Bring to a boil, lower heat and simmer, uncovered, for 15 minutes.

Preheat oven to 325°.

Cover baking pan and set in the oven. Immediately lower oven temperature to 300°. Cook until meat is just tender, about 1 1/2 hours. Add the onions, carrots and green beans and continue cooking until vegetables are tender, about 45 minutes longer. Adjust seasoning with salt and pepper.

6 servings

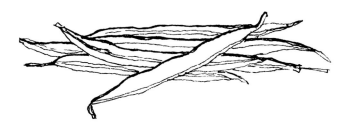

$\mathcal{M}$eatballs in White Sauce

1/2 pound each of ground beef,
  pork, veal
2 cups whole wheat bread, cubed
1/2 cup milk
10 tablespoons lightly salted
  butter
1 onion, finely chopped
2 teaspoons salt
2 teaspoons paprika

1 teaspoon poultry seasoning
1/4 teaspoon dry mustard
1/4 teaspoon pepper
3 eggs, beaten
1/4 cup flour
1 tablespoon tomato paste
a 13 3/4-ounce can beef broth
1 cup sour cream

In a bowl combine the beef, pork and veal.

In another bowl soak the bread cubes in milk. Squeeze dry and add to the meat.

In a saucepan melt 2 tablespoons of the butter and sauté the onion until it is soft. Add to the meat mixture.

Stir in the salt, paprika, poultry seasoning, mustard, pepper and eggs. Mix well and form into small balls. Mixture will be moist.

Heat the remaining butter in a saucepan and brown the meatballs, being careful they do not touch. Remove as they cook. When all the meatballs are browned, stir the flour into the pan drippings. Combine the tomato paste with the broth and mix with enough water to make 2 1/4 cups. Add to the flour and stir over low heat until sauce is thickened. Return the meatballs to the saucepan and heat through.

Before serving, stir in the sour cream, blending well.

6 to 8 servings

$\mathscr{M}$eat Roll with Cheese and Ham

2 eggs, beaten
1/2 cup tomato juice
3/4 cup soft bread crumbs
2 tablespoons chopped fresh
   parsley
1/2 teaspoon dried oregano
1/4 teaspoon salt

1/4 teaspoon pepper
1 clove garlic, minced
1 pound ground beef
1/2 pound ground veal
1/2 pound ground pork
4 ounces boiled ham, thinly sliced
6 ounces mozzarella cheese,
   grated

Preheat oven to 350°.

In a bowl combine the eggs and tomato juice. Stir in the bread crumbs, parsley, oregano, salt and pepper and garlic. Add the meat and mix well.

On wax paper, pat the meat into a 10x8-inch rectangle. Arrange ham slices on top of meat, leaving a small margin around the edges. Sprinkle mozzarella cheese over ham, reserving 2 tablespoons for the top. Starting from the short end, carefully roll up the meat, using the wax paper to lift. Seal edge and ends. Place roll, seam side down, in a 13x9x2-inch baking pan. Bake until done, about 1 1/4 hours. (Center of roll will be pink because of the ham.) Sprinkle remaining cheese on top. Return to the oven until the cheese melts, about 2 minutes.

8 servings

175

aked Corned Beef

1 corned beef
1 clove garlic, crushed
2 onions each studded with 2
   whole cloves

1 bay leaf
ground cloves
Basting Sauce

In a deep saucepan combine the corned beef, garlic, onion and bay leaf and cover with water. Follow cooking directions on back of corned beef package.

Preheat oven to 350°.

Transfer corned beef to a roasting pan and sprinkle with the ground cloves. Bake for 30 minutes, basting occasionally with the Basting Sauce.

Basting Sauce
2 tablespoons unsalted butter
1/3 cup brown sugar
1 tablespoon Dijon mustard

1/3 cup ketchup
3 tablespoons red wine vinegar

In a small saucepan combine all the ingredients and heat thoroughly.

4 to 6 servings

Deviled Short Ribs

3 pounds beef short ribs

Marinade

3/4 cup dry red wine
1/4 cup olive oil
2 tablespoons Dijon mustard
2 tablespoons white wine vinegar
1 onion, sliced thinly

1 clove garlic, minced
1 teaspoon sugar
1/4 teaspoon dried thyme
1 bay leaf
salt and pepper to taste

Must be prepared in advance.

In a large bowl combine all the ingredients. Add the short ribs, turning them to coat, and marinate, turning occasionally, for 3 hours or overnight. Remove the ribs and set aside. Strain the marinade through a fine sieve into a saucepan and reduce it over moderately high heat to about 3/4 cup.

1/4 cup vegetable oil
3 onions, chopped

2 cups beef broth
salt and pepper to taste

Preheat oven to 300°.

In a saucepan just large enough to hold the short ribs in one layer heat the oil over moderately high heat and quickly brown the ribs. Transfer them to a plate. In the same saucepan cook the onions, stirring until they are golden. Return the ribs to the saucepan and add the reduced Marinade and enough of the broth to half cover the ribs. Bring the liquid to a boil, cover and place in the oven. Cook, turning ribs 2 or 3 times, until they are tender, about 2 hours. Transfer the ribs to a platter and keep them warm.
    Remove the onions and set aside. Skim fat from the cooking liquid.
    In a saucepan bring the cooking liquid to a boil and boil until it is reduced to about 1 1/2 cups.
    In a food processor, puree the onions. Combine with the cooking liquid. Adjust seasoning with salt and pepper. Spoon some of the sauce over the ribs and serve the remaining sauce separately.

4 servings

DINNER BY THE FIRESIDE

It's a far cry from the steamy courts of Wimbledon and a hurried sip of cool water between sets, but here at the home of League member Patti Graebner, her husband, well-known tennis star Clark Graebner has a much deserved opportunity to sit back comfortably and enjoy the pleasures of a busy and successful life.

Marinades for Spareribs or Steak

Marinade 1
1 teaspoon salt
3 tablespoons soy sauce
2 tablespoons sherry

4 tablespoons hoisin sauce
5 cloves garlic, finely minced
2 teaspoons sugar

Marinade 2
6 scallions, finely chopped
5 cloves garlic, crushed
1/2 cup soy sauce
2 tablespoons vegetable oil
2 tablespoons dry sherry

2 tablespoons firmly packed
  brown sugar
2 tablespoons sesame seeds,
  toasted
pepper to taste

Marinade 3
1/2 cup soy sauce
3 tablespoons vegetable oil
3 tablespoons honey

1 teaspoon minced fresh ginger
1 clove garlic, crushed

Marinade 4
1/2 cup ketchup
dash of Tabasco sauce
1 tablespoon Worcestershire
  sauce
1 onion, grated

1/4 cup white vinegar
1 clove garlic, crushed
1 teaspoon pepper
1 teaspoon salt
1/4 cup sugar

For each marinade, combine all the ingredients in a small saucepan and simmer, uncovered, for 5 minutes.

2 pounds spareribs

Slice the spareribs between the ribs. Marinate for one hour at room temperature or longer in the refrigerator.
Preheat oven to 350°. Bake 40 to 50 minutes, basting frequently.

a 1 1/2-pound flank steak

Pour the marinade over the steak. Marinate for one hour at room temperature or longer in the refrigerator, turning occasionally.
Broil steak about 5 minutes on each side, basting frequently. Cut diagonally into thin slices.

a 2-pound boneless sirloin steak

Cut steak into 1/2-inch thick slices across the grain. Marinate for one hour at room temperature or longer in the refrigerator, turning occasionally.
Broil steak to desired degree of doneness.

Roast Veal with Tomato Sage Relish

a 3 3/4-pound boned veal roast
1/2 cup Niçoise olives, pitted and
  slivered
3 garlic cloves, slivered
1/4 cup olive oil

salt and pepper to taste
1 1/2 cups chicken broth
1 1/2 cups dry white wine
1 lemon
Tomato Sage Relish

Preheat oven to 325°.

Pat veal dry. Pierce holes all over with the point of a knife and insert the olives and garlic.

In a skillet heat the oil and brown the veal on all sides. Transfer the veal to a rack in a roasting pan. Set aside the skillet and the drippings for the Relish. Season meat with salt and pepper. Roast veal until tender, about 2 hours.

Combine the broth and wine. Baste the meat with 1/3 cup of the broth every 20 minutes. Squeeze half of the lemon over veal at the start of the roasting time and the remaining lemon a half hour before veal is cooked. Add more broth mixture to pan if necessary to keep bottom of pan covered. Slice the veal and transfer to a serving platter. Place the Tomato Sage Relish in the center.

Tomato Sage Relish
2 tablespoons olive oil
1 large onion, thinly sliced
3 teaspoons minced garlic

2 1/2 pounds tomatoes, peeled,
  seeded, chopped and drained
salt and white pepper to taste
1/8 teaspoon dried sage

In the skillet with the veal drippings add enough oil to measure 3 tablespoons. Heat the oil and sauté the onion and garlic for 4 minutes. Stir the tomatoes into the onion mixture. Reduce the pan juices to a quarter cup, scraping up any browned particles. Add to the tomato mixture. Simmer, stirring occasionally, until mixture is thick, about 5 minutes. Adjust seasoning with salt and pepper. Cool. Mix in the sage.

8 servings

Stuffed Veal Roast

Contributed by Chef Marc Colle, Il Villano, Westport

a 2-pound boneless breast of veal
4 pounds fresh spinach, washed
   and coarsely chopped
1/2 cup grated Parmesan cheese
1 clove garlic, finely minced
a pinch of dried rosemary

pepper to taste
2 carrots, cut into 1-inch pieces
2 small potatoes, cut into 1-inch
   cubes
2 onions, cut into 1-inch cubes
fresh parsley for garnish

Preheat oven to 350°. Butter a 12-inch roasting pan.

In a bowl combine the spinach, Parmesan cheese, garlic, rosemary and pepper. Spread the spinach mixture over the veal, roll and tie with string. Place the veal in the prepared pan and surround it with the vegetables. Roast until golden brown, about 45 minutes, basting occasionally. Cut veal roast into 1 1/2-inch slices, transfer to a serving platter and garnish with the cooked vegetables and parsley.

4 servings

Baked Veal Chops with Rice

4 veal chops
4 tablespoons (1/2 stick) unsalted
   butter
3/4 cup rice

1 medium onion, sliced
a 13 3/4-ounce can beef broth
1/2 cup white wine

Preheat oven to 350°.

In a saucepan melt 2 tablespoons of the butter and sauté the veal until browned on both sides. Remove with a slotted spoon.

In the same saucepan melt the remaining 2 tablespoons butter and lightly brown the rice. Transfer the rice to a baking dish large enough to hold the veal chops in one layer. Place the chops on top of the rice and cover with the onion slices. Pour broth and wine over all.

Cover and bake for 45 minutes. Remove cover and bake 15 minutes longer.

4 servings

range Veal Piccata

1 pound veal scallops, cut 1/8-inch thick
1/2 cup flour
salt and pepper to taste
4 tablespoons (1/2 stick) unsalted butter

2 teaspoons vegetable oil
1 cup orange juice
1/8 teaspoon dried sage, crumbled
1 tablespoon unsalted butter
minced fresh parsley for garnish

Season flour with salt and pepper and dust veal lightly.

In a saucepan heat the 4 tablespoons of butter with the oil and quickly sauté the veal 30 seconds on each side. Do not crowd. Transfer to a plate and keep warm.

Discard pan drippings. Add 1/2 cup orange juice to saucepan and boil until reduced to a glaze, scraping up browned particles, about 1 minute. Add remaining orange juice and sage. Season with salt and pepper. Boil until mixture thickens and just coats spoon, about 1 minute. Remove from heat and swirl in the 1 tablespoon of butter. Pour in any juices accumulated from veal. Spoon sauce over. Sprinkle with parsley.

4 servings

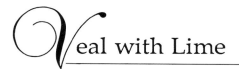eal with Lime

2 pounds veal scallops, pounded
1/3 cup flour
1 teaspoon salt
1/2 teaspoon white pepper
1/2 teaspoon dried tarragon

3 tablespoons unsalted butter
1 tablespoon oil
1/2 cup dry white wine
1 cup crème fraîche
3 tablespoons fresh lime juice

Season the flour with the salt, pepper and tarragon and dust veal lightly.

In a saucepan heat the butter with the oil and brown the veal on both sides. Transfer to a heated platter.

In the same saucepan discard any remaining butter and add the wine, scraping loose the browned particles. Over high heat reduce the wine by two-thirds. Lower the heat and add the crème fraîche. Cook until reduced by half. Stir in the lime juice and any accumulated juices from the veal. Return the veal to the saucepan and heat.

4 to 6 servings

Veal Rolls with Tarragon

6 veal scallops, lightly pounded
salt and pepper to taste
2 tablespoons unsalted butter
3 tablespoons olive oil
3/4 cup fresh bread crumbs
1 clove garlic, minced
1 tablespoon grated Parmesan
  cheese

1/4 cup finely chopped fresh
  parsley
grated rind of 1 lemon
1 teaspoon dried tarragon
3 tablespoons heavy cream
1 tablespoon flour
1 cup chicken broth
1 tablespoon lemon juice.

Preheat oven to 350°.

Salt and pepper the scallops.

In a small saucepan melt the butter and mix in the bread crumbs, garlic, Parmesan cheese, parsley, lemon rind, tarragon, cream and salt and pepper. Divide the mixture among the 6 scallops. Roll up each slice and secure with a toothpick.

In another saucepan heat the oil and sauté the veal rolls until browned on all sides. Transfer veal rolls to a baking dish.

Sprinkle the flour over the fat remaining in the saucepan and cook briefly. Add the broth and stir to dissolve the browned particles in the bottom of the saucepan. Add the lemon juice and bring to a boil. Pour the sauce over the veal. Cover and bake 45 minutes.

6 servings

Veal with Mushrooms

4 veal scallops, pounded
4 slices Swiss cheese
4 tablespoons flour
4 tablespoons (1/2 stick) unsalted
  butter

1/4 pound mushrooms, sliced
1/4 cup Scotch whiskey
2 cups heavy cream

Place one slice of Swiss cheese on each scallop. Roll up scallops and secure with toothpicks. Dust with the flour.

In a saucepan melt the butter and sauté the veal rolls. Add the mushrooms and cook 5 minutes. Remove from heat.

Sprinkle veal with the Scotch and flame 1 minute. Cover pan to extinguish flames. Gently blend in the cream and simmer until slightly thickened, about 5 minutes.

4 servings

ork in Bourbon

a 3-pound boneless loin of pork
2/3 cup Dijon mustard
1/2 cup brown sugar
3 tablespoons oil

1/3 cup Bourbon whiskey
a bouquet garni in cheesecloth bag
  (thyme, oregano, parsley)
2/3 cup beef broth

Preheat oven to 375°.

Spread the mustard on the pork and roll in the brown sugar.
In a saucepan heat the oil and sauté the pork until browned.
Pour Bourbon on top and flame 1 minute. Cover the pan to
extinguish flames.
Place in a baking dish, add the bouquet garni and broth, cover
and bake 1 1/2 hours, skimming off fat as it accumulates.
Serve with pan juices.

6 servings

ork Chops with Currants

4 loin pork chops
1 tablespoon vegetable oil
2 large onions, quartered
salt and pepper to taste

1 cup chicken broth
1/2 cup white wine
1 teaspoon dried thyme
1/2 cup currants

In a saucepan heat the oil and brown the chops with the onion.
Add salt and pepper. Pour broth and wine over chops and add
the thyme and currants. Bring to a boil, lower heat and simmer
for one hour, adding more broth, if necessary. If too much liquid
is left at the end of one hour, remove chops and boil liquid until
it is reduced to gravy consistency. Spoon pan liquids over chops.

4 servings

185

$\mathcal{S}$tuffed Pork Roast with Two Sauces

a 4-pound center cut pork loin, boned   Onion Cream Sauce
Pecan Bread Stuffing   Cranberry Coulis

Preheat oven to 400°.

Spread a quarter of the stuffing over the pork loin, roll and tie with string. Spoon remaining stuffing into a baking dish, cover and set aside.

Place the roast on a rack in a shallow roasting pan. Set roast in oven and immediately lower temperature to 350°. Roast until meat thermometer inserted in thickest part of the meat registers 160°, about 1 1/2 hours. Remove the roast from the oven. Let stand 15 minutes before carving.

Bake stuffing for 30 minutes.

Cut roast into slices. (Stuffing will probably slip out.) Center stuffing on each dinner plate and place 2 slices of pork over top, covering stuffing completely.

Serve with Onion Cream Sauce and Cranberry Coulis.

Pecan Bread Stuffing

8 tablespoons (1 stick) unsalted   1/2 cup French bread, crusts
  butter   trimmed
1 1/2 pounds onions, thinly sliced   1 teaspoon salt
1 cup pecans, toasted   1/4 teaspoon pepper
2 ounces prosciutto ham

In a saucepan heat the butter and sauté the onions until they are very soft, about 30 minutes. Transfer half of the onion to a food processor, reserving the remaining onion for Onion Cream Sauce. Add the pecans, prosciutto ham, bread and salt and pepper and mince. Adjust seasoning with salt and pepper. Chill before using.

Onion Cream Sauce

2 cups whipping cream   onion reserved from stuffing
1/2 cup beef broth   salt and white pepper to taste

In a saucepan combine the cream, broth and onion and cook, stirring occasionally, until mixture is reduced to 2 1/2 cups, about 30 minutes. Let cool slightly. Transfer to a food processor and puree. Strain puree into bowl, discarding any unblended bits of onion. Stir in salt and pepper to taste.

Before serving, heat through.

Cranberry Coulis

1 cup water
1/2 cup sugar
1 pound cranberries

3/4 teaspoon salt
1/4 teaspoon pepper

In a saucepan combine the water and sugar and bring to a boil, making sure sugar is dissolved. Add the cranberries. Lower heat, cover and simmer until cranberries have popped, about 5 minutes. Transfer to a food processor and puree. Strain through a sieve. Stir in salt and pepper. Before serving, heat through.

8 servings

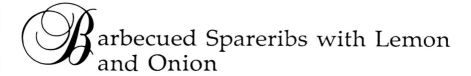arbecued Spareribs with Lemon and Onion

2 1/2 pounds spareribs
1 onion, sliced
1 lemon, sliced

1/3 cup Worcestershire sauce
2 cups water
1 cup ketchup

Preheat oven to 400°.

Place spareribs in a shallow roasting pan. Arrange onion and lemon slices on top. Cook for 1/2 hour. Drain fat.

In a bowl combine the Worcestershire sauce, water and ketchup. Pour over the spareribs and continue cooking one hour longer, adding more water if necessary.

4 servings

am Steak

a 3/4-inch thick ham steak
1 1/2 tablespoons unsalted butter
3/4 cup grated Parmesan cheese
3/4 cup grated Gruyère cheese

1 teaspoon Dijon mustard
1/3 cup heavy cream
  (approximately)

Preheat broiler.

In a large saucepan melt the butter and briefly cook the ham on both sides until heated through. Transfer to a shallow baking dish.
In a bowl combine the Parmesan cheese and the Gruyère cheese with the mustard and beat in just enough heavy cream to make a thick but spreadable paste.
Spread mixture evenly over ham and broil until the cheese is melted and top is browned.

4 servings

ielbasa with Potatoes

1 pound kielbasa sausage
2 pounds cooked potatoes, cut into
  1/2-inch thick slices
4 hard-cooked eggs, sliced

8 tablespoons (1 stick) unsalted
  butter, melted
2 cups sour cream, thinned with 2
  tablespoons milk
salt and pepper to taste

Preheat oven to 350°. Butter an ovenproof baking dish.

Poach kielbasa in boiling water to soften skin. Remove and peel casing. Cut into 1/2-inch thick slices.

To assemble:
Alternate layers of potato, egg and kielbasa, sprinkling each layer with butter and sour cream and ending with a layer of potato. Season with salt and pepper.
Bake until delicately browned, about one hour.

4 servings

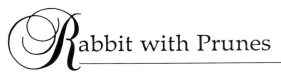

Rabbit with Prunes

2 1/2 pounds rabbit, cut into
   serving pieces
1/2 cup chopped carrot
1/2 cup chopped onion
1/2 cup chopped celery
1/4 cup red wine vinegar
2 cups dry red wine
2 parsley sprigs
1/2 teaspoon dried thyme

1 bay leaf
salt and pepper to taste
2 tablespoons olive oil
2 tablespoons unsalted butter
2 tablespoons flour
1/3 cup chicken broth
1/2 pound pitted dried prunes,
   halved

Must be prepared a day in advance.

In a bowl combine the rabbit, carrot, onion, celery, vinegar, wine, parsley, thyme, bay leaf and salt and pepper. Cover and refrigerate overnight, turning occasionally.

Discard the parsley and bay leaf. Remove the rabbit. Drain the vegetables and set aside. Reserve the marinade.

In a heavy saucepan heat the oil and butter. Add the rabbit and brown on all sides. Add the reserved vegetables. Stir and cook briefly. Skim off any fat.

Sprinkle the flour on top of the rabbit, stirring to mix with the vegetables. Add the reserved marinade and broth. Bring to a boil, lower heat and simmer 20 minutes. Add the prunes and cook, covered, for 20 minutes longer.

Recipe can be doubled.

4 servings

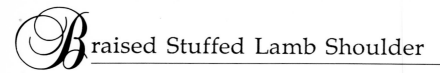raised Stuffed Lamb Shoulder

a 5–pound lamb shoulder, boned and bones reserved

Stuffing

2 tablespoons unsalted butter
1 medium onion, finely chopped
1 cup long grain rice
2 cups water
1/2 cup currants

salt and pepper to taste
1/2 cup pine nuts, lightly toasted
2 tablespoons chopped fresh
  parsley
2 eggs

In a saucepan melt the butter and sauté the onion until soft but not brown. Add the rice and cook stirring, until the grains are transparent. Add the water, currants, salt and pepper and cover. Bring to a boil, lower heat and simmer for exactly 18 minutes. Let stand 10 minutes to cool before removing cover. Stir to separate the grains and let cool. Stir in the pine nuts, parsley and eggs, one at a time. Spoon the Stuffing into the middle of the butterflied lamb and sew up with string to a cushion shape. *Can be prepared up to 5 hours in advance up to this point.*

1 tablespoon butter, melted
1 onion, quartered
1 carrot, quartered
1-2 cloves garlic, peeled and cut
  in slivers

1 teaspoon dried rosemary
salt and pepper to taste
1/2 cup white wine
1 cup beef broth

Preheat oven to 400°.

In a roasting pan combine the butter, lamb bones, onion and carrot. Make several incisions in the meat with the point of a knife and insert the garlic slivers. Sprinkle the meat with rosemary and salt and pepper. Place the lamb on top of the vegetables and bones and cook, basting often, for 1 1/4 to 1 1/2 hours. Remove excess fat, if necessary.

Transfer the lamb to a platter and let rest 15 minutes before carving. Discard the excess fat from the pan but leave in the bones, onion and carrot. Add the wine and reduce over high heat by half. Add the broth and simmer briefly. Strain into a small saucepan, discarding the solids. Bring back to a boil and adjust the seasoning with salt and pepper. Serve separately.

6 servings

arinated Lamb

a leg of lamb (6-7 pounds), boned and butterflied

Must be prepared in advance.

Marinade 1 ✕
1 clove garlic, crushed
3/4 cup olive oil
1/4 cup red wine vinegar
1/2 cup chopped onion
2 teaspoons Dijon mustard

1/2 teaspoon dried oregano
1/2 teaspoon dried basil
1 bay leaf, crushed
salt and pepper to taste

Marinade 2
1/2 cup Dijon mustard
2 tablespoons soy sauce
1 teaspoon dried rosemary

1/2 teaspoon ground ginger
1 clove garlic, minced
2 tablespoons olive oil

Marinade 3
1 onion, minced
1 teaspoon grated ginger
3 cloves garlic, minced
1/2 cup lemon juice
2 teaspoons ground coriander

2 teaspoons curry powder
1/8 teaspoon each of ground mace,
   nutmeg, cinnamon, ground cloves
1 cup olive oil
salt and pepper to taste

For each marinade combine all the ingredients in a small bowl. Pour the marinade over the lamb, turning to coat. Cover and refrigerate overnight, turning occasionally.

Remove the lamb from the refrigerator about one hour before cooking.

Preheat broiler.

Place the meat with the marinade in a roasting pan, fat side up. Broil about 4 inches from the heat for 10 minutes. Turn, baste and broil 10 minutes on the other side. Transfer the meat to the middle of the oven and set oven temperature to 425°. Roast about 15 minutes. or more!

Carve the lamb into thin slices.

Lamb chops — 3" from heat,
broil 5 min ea. side   6 servings

$\mathcal{L}$amb Curry

2 pounds lean lamb, cubed	1/2 teaspoon ground ginger
2 tablespoons oil	2 tomatoes, peeled and chopped
1 cup onion, chopped	1/4 cup water
1 clove garlic, minced	3 tablespoons flour
1-2 tablespoons curry powder	salt and pepper to taste

In a saucepan heat the oil and brown the lamb on all sides. Remove lamb with a slotted spoon. In the same saucepan, sauté the onion and garlic until tender but not browned.

Return the lamb to the saucepan and stir in the curry powder, ginger, tomatoes and water. Cover and simmer, stirring occasionally, until lamb is tender, about 50 minutes. Stir in the flour and cook until thickened. Adjust the seasoning with salt and pepper.

4 servings

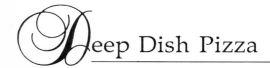eep Dish Pizza

Dough

1 package dry yeast	1 teaspoon salt
1 cup lukewarm water	2 tablespoons oil
1 tablespoon sugar	2 1/2 - 3 cups flour

In a food processor dissolve the yeast in water, add the sugar, salt and oil and mix. While processor is running, gradually add the flour. As soon as a ball forms on top of the processor blade, stop machine and remove dough. Knead on floured surface until smooth and elastic. Place in a lightly oiled bowl, cover and let rise in a warm place, about two hours.

Meat Sauce

1 pound Italian sausage	6 ounces tomato paste
1/4 cup chopped onion	1/2 pound mushrooms, sliced
1 clove garlic, minced	1 teaspoon dried oregano
a 14-ounce can imported tomatoes	1 teaspoon salt
with juice, chopped	1/8 teaspoon pepper

Remove sausage casings. In a saucepan sauté the sausage, crumbling with a fork. Add the onion and garlic and cook until the onion is soft. Drain all the pan juices. Add the remaining ingredients to the sausage mixture. Simmer for 30 minutes and let cool.

Cheese Filling

1 pound ricotta cheese	2 eggs, lightly beaten
1/4 pound mozzarella cheese, grated	1/4 cup chopped fresh parsley
	1/8 teaspoon salt

In a large bowl combine all the ingredients and mix well. Set aside.

Topping

1/2 pound mozzarella cheese, grated	1/2 teaspoon dried oregano
	1/4 cup grated Parmesan cheese.

Preheat oven to 400°.

To assemble:
Roll out half of the Dough to fit a 10x13-inch baking pan. Spread Cheese Filling on top of the dough. Roll out remaining dough and place over Cheese Filling. Top with Meat Sauce and bake for 15 minutes. Remove from oven and sprinkle with the Topping. Return to oven and bake until top is golden, about 15 more minutes.

6 to 8 servings

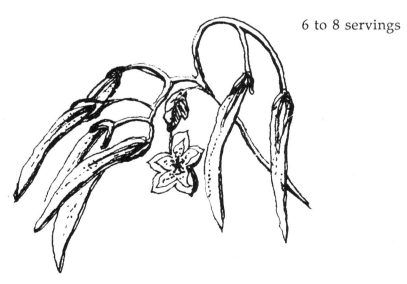

Venison with Potatoes

6 pounds leg of venison, cut into
   serving pieces
Marinade to cover
1/4 cup olive oil
1/4 cup cognac, warmed
1 tablespoon tomato paste

1 bay leaf
3/4 cup flour
1 bottle red wine
2 cups of the Marinade
salt and pepper to taste
boiled potatoes

Must be made two days in advance.

In a glass bowl combine the meat and Marinade, cover and refrigerate for two days, turning occasionally.

Pat meat dry with paper towels.

In a heavy skillet heat the oil and brown the venison. Add the vegetables from the Marinade and the cognac. Flame for one minute. Add the tomato paste, bay leaf and flour and stir well to mix with the meat. Add the wine and 2 cups of the Marinade. Transfer to a large saucepan, cover and simmer until meat is tender, about 1 1/2 hours.

Remove meat to a warm serving platter. Strain the stock and adjust seasoning with salt and pepper. Pour over the meat and arrange the boiled potatoes all around.

Marinade
1 onion, chopped
2 carrots, chopped
2 cloves garlic, crushed
2 bay leaves
1 teaspoon dried thyme

2 tablespoons red vinegar
1/2 cup olive oil
2 tablespoons salt
1 teaspoon pepper
1 bottle red Burgundy wine

Mix all ingredients together.

LUNCHEON BY LONGSHORE

Among the many landmarks in Westport is the Inn at Longshore. Situated along Long Island Sound, Longshore is a town-owned facility that was once a private country club. Westporters enjoy its sailing, golf, tennis, and swimming facilities. The Inn has been restored and is a favored dining spot, especially on warm summer evenings, where visitors enjoy the water view. The Inn at Longshore has been the site of many League functions, including a spectacular Roaring Twenties Casino Night and a favorite League function, the mid-winter gala.

$\mathcal{L}$inguine with Red Clam Sauce

1 pound linguine
two 6 1/2-ounce cans minced clams
1/2 cup olive oil
2 large cloves garlic, minced
1/2 teaspoon dried thyme

6 tablespoons chopped fresh
  parsley
2 cups Tomato Sauce
salt and pepper to taste
12 little neck clams

Cook the linguine in lightly salted water, al dente.

In a saucepan heat the oil and briefly sauté the garlic. Do not let it brown. Add the remaining ingredients and simmer for 5 minutes. Add the fresh clams and bring to a boil. Cook until the clams open. Discard any that do not open. Serve over the linguine.

Tomato Sauce
4 tablespoons olive oil
1 1/2 cups finely chopped onion
2 cloves garlic, finely chopped
a 35-ounce can Italian plum
  tomatoes
a 6-ounce can tomato paste
1 1/2 cups water

salt and pepper to taste
1/2 teaspoon sugar
1/2 teaspoon dried thyme
1 teaspoon dried basil
1 bay leaf
1 tablespoon finely chopped fresh
  parsley

In a saucepan heat the oil and sauté the onion and garlic until the onion is soft. Add the remaining ingredients and simmer, stirring occasionally, about 30 minutes. *Can be made in advance and frozen.*

6 servings

Pasta Provençal

3 tablespoons olive oil
1 tablespoon unsalted butter
6 cups onion, very thinly sliced
5 cloves garlic, minced
3/4 cup white wine
1 1/4 cup chicken broth

6 large tomatoes, peeled, seeded
  and coarsely chopped
1/4 cup finely chopped fresh
  parsley
salt and pepper to taste
1 pound *fresh* linguine

In a large saucepan heat the oil with the butter and sauté the onion over medium high heat for 5 minutes. Lower heat, add the garlic and sauté, stirring frequently, until the onions are lightly browned, about 10 minutes.

Add the wine to the onion and bring the mixture to a boil. Let the liquid reduce until it is almost completely evaporated. Add the chicken broth and the tomatoes. Simmer until the sauce is very thick, about 30 minutes.

Add the parsley, salt and pepper and simmer for a few more minutes.

Cook the linguine in lightly salted boiling water, al dente. Drain well and transfer to a large bowl. Add the sauce and mix gently.

4 servings

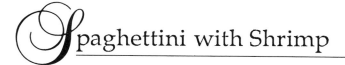
Spaghettini with Shrimp

1 pound spaghettini
6 tablespoons (3/4 stick) unsalted
  butter
1 clove garlic, crushed
1 pound shrimp, shelled and
  deveined

1 cup sliced fresh mushrooms
juice of 2 lemons
1/2 cup dry white wine
1/2 cup grated Parmesan cheese

Cook pasta is lightly salted water, al dente. Drain and cool.

In a saucepan melt 4 tablespoons of the butter and briefly sauté garlic to flavor the butter. Add the shrimp and cook until they turn pink, about 5 minutes. Remove shrimp with a slotted spoon.

In the same saucepan add the remaining 2 tablespoons butter and sauté the mushrooms. Add the lemon juice and wine. Heat thoroughly and return the shrimp to the pan. Add the Parmesan cheese and toss to mix. Pour immediately over pasta.

6 servings

Tomato and Fettucine Salad

6 ounces fettucine, cut in half
1/4 cup pitted black olives, sliced
1/4 cup pitted green olives, sliced
1 tablespoon capers
4 large tomatoes, seeded, peeled and chopped

1/4 cup chopped fresh parsley
2 tablespoons wine vinegar
4 tablespoons olive oil
2 tablespoons finely chopped fresh basil
salt and pepper to taste

Must be prepared in advance.

Cook pasta in lightly salted boiling water, al dente.
Meanwhile, combine all the remaining ingredients and mix well. Set aside.
Pour sauce over fettucine and toss until well combined. Refrigerate for one to two hours.
Before serving, bring to room temperature and toss again.

6 servings

Shrimp and Spaghetti Salad

12 ounces spaghetti, broken in half
1/4 cup bottled Italian dressing
1 pound cooked shrimp, deveined and cut in half lengthwise
4 hard-cooked eggs, chopped
1 cup broccoli florets
1 small zucchini, coarsely chopped

6 scallions, chopped
6 radishes, sliced
1 green pepper, chopped
3 stalks celery, chopped
2 tablespoons pimiento, chopped
4 tablespoons pickle relish
1 1/3 cups mayonnaise
lemon pepper to taste

Must be made in advance.

Cook spaghetti in lightly salted water, al dente. Drain and cool. Transfer to a bowl and pour the Italian dressing. Add the remaining ingredients except the lemon pepper and toss lightly.
Season to taste using generous amounts of lemon pepper and mix together lightly. Cover and refrigerate several hours before serving.

8 servings

$\mathcal{L}$inguine with Broccoli, Tomato and Walnuts

1 medium bunch broccoli, cut into
1 1/2-inch pieces (6 cups)
1 pound *fresh* linguine
4 tablespoons (1/2 stick) unsalted
butter
2 tablespoons olive oil
1 pint cherry tomatoes
1 large clove garlic, minced

pinch red pepper flakes
1 teaspoon dried basil
1/2-1 cup chicken broth
1/2 cup grated Parmesan cheese
1/4 cup chopped fresh parsley
1/2 cup coarsely chopped
walnuts, lightly toasted

Cook the broccoli in lightly salted water for 5 minutes. Add the linguine and cook for 2 minutes. Drain and set aside.

Meanwhile, in a saucepan melt 2 tablespoons of the butter and the oil over moderate heat. Add the tomatoes and cook, stirring frequently until tomatoes are tender but still hold their shape, about 3 minutes. Stir in the garlic, pepper flakes and basil and cook 1 minute longer. Remove from heat, cover to keep warm.

In the saucepan in which the pasta was cooked, melt the remaining 2 tablespoons of butter and return the linguine and broccoli to the saucepan. Toss to coat with the butter. Add the tomatoes, 1/2 cup of the broth, the Parmesan cheese and parsley. Toss to blend, adding more broth if mixture seems dry.

Transfer to a bowl and garnish with the walnuts.

4 to 6 servings

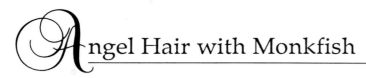# ngel Hair with Monkfish

Contributed by The Pompano Grille, Westport

1 pound whole wheat vermicelli
   or packaged angel hair
6 monkfish medallions
18 shrimp, cleaned and deveined
24 sea scallops
flour
3 tablespoons oil
1 cup broccoli florets
1 cup julienne carrots

an 8-ounce can sliced water
   chestnuts, drained and rinsed
an 8-ounce can sliced bamboo
   shoots, drained and rinsed
1 cup cherry tomatoes, halved
6 scallions, finely chopped
1 1/2 tablespoons cornstarch
   mixed with 2 tablespoons water
Pineapple Soy Sauce

Cook the vermicelli in lightly salted water, al dente.

Lightly coat the monkfish and shrimp with the flour.

In a large skillet heat 2 tablespoons of the oil and sauté the monkfish, shrimp and scallops until partially cooked. Remove from pan and set aside.

In another saucepan heat the remaining tablespoon of oil and briefly sauté all the vegetables, about 3 to 4 minutes. Return the seafood to the pan and add the Pineapple Soy Sauce. Bring to a boil, lower heat and simmer, uncovered, until seafood is cooked, about 5 minutes. Slowly stir in the cornstarch mixture, adding only enough to thicken sauce to taste. Serve over the pasta.

Pineapple Soy Sauce
3/4 cup soy sauce
1/2 cup honey
1/2 cup dry sherry
1 clove garlic, minced

1 cup plus 2 tablespoons water
1/2 cup pineapple juice
1/4 teaspoon minced fresh ginger

Combine all the ingredients.

6 servings

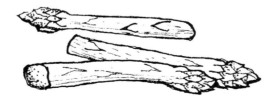

asta Primavera

7 tablespoons olive oil
1 medium onion, minced
1 large garlic clove, minced
3 tablespoons minced fresh
  parsley
1/4 cup minced fresh basil
2 ounces prosciutto ham, chopped
5 scallions, chopped
1 cup petit peas, frozen and
  thawed
1/2 pound asparagus, cut
  diagonally into 1/4-inch slices
1 medium zucchini, quartered
  lengthwise and sliced 1/4-inch
  thick

1 small carrot, halved
  lengthwise, cut diagonally 1/8-
  inch thick
1 cup broccoli florets
1 cup snow peas, trimmed and
  halved
1 pound spaghetti
1/2 pound fresh mushrooms,
  thinly sliced
1/2 cup chicken broth
6 tablespoons unsalted butter
1 cup heavy cream
1 1/2 cups grated Parmesan cheese
  to taste
salt and pepper to taste

In a small saucepan heat 3 tablespoons of the oil and sauté the onion and garlic until the onion is softened, about 2 minutes. Add the parsley and basil. Stir in the prosciutto, scallions and peas and cook 1 minute longer. Set aside.

Meanwhile, in a large kettle bring to a boil 5 quarts of water. Add the asparagus, zucchini, carrot, broccoli and snow peas and bring to a rolling boil. Cook 1 minute and remove the vegetables with a sieve. Run cold water over them until they are thoroughly cooled. Spread vegetables on paper towels to dry. Reserve the pot of water. *Can be made in advance up to this point.*

Return the pot of water to a boil. Add the spaghetti and cook, al dente.

Meanwhile, in a saucepan heat the remaining 4 tablespoons of oil and add the mushrooms. Sauté, stirring occasionally for a few minutes, until the mushrooms are very lightly colored. Add the cooked green vegetables and toss over high heat until most of the liquid has evaporated and the vegetables are barely tender. Set aside.

When the spaghetti is done, drain well, return it to the pot and add the chicken broth and the reserved onion mixture. Over low heat add the butter, cream and the Parmesan cheese. Stir with a fork until the cheese melts.

Add the vegetable mushroom mixture to the spaghetti and mix well. Adjust seasoning with salt and pepper.

8 to 10 servings

Cold Noodles with Sesame Sauce

1 pound Chinese noodles or
  vermicelli
3/4 cup tahini (sesame seed
  paste)
1 cup water
1/4 tablespoons soy sauce
2 tablespoon Chinese vinegar
2 tablespoon sugar
1 teaspoon hot chili oil

a 1-inch piece fresh ginger
2 tablespoons Oriental sesame oil
2 cloves garlic
1 cooked chicken breast, boned
  and cut into slivers
1 cucumber, peeled, halved
  lengthwise, seeded and sliced
  thinly into crescents
1 bunch scallions, finely chopped

Cook the noodles in lightly salted water, al dente. Drain and cool under cold running water.

In a food processor add the remaining ingredients except the chicken, cucumber and scallions and blend well. *Can be made in advance up to this point.*

In a large bowl combine the noodles with the sesame sauce, chicken and cucumber. Toss well. Transfer to a serving platter. Sprinkle the scallions on top.

6 to 8 servings

Pasta and Eggplant

1/4 cup olive oil
2 cloves garlic, coarsely chopped
a 2-ounce can anchovy fillets
  with oil
two 28-ounce cans crushed Italian
  tomatoes
2 fresh basil leaves
salt and pepper to taste

1/2 cup vegetable oil
2 eggplants (about 3 pounds), cut
  into 1-inch cubes
1 1/2 cups pitted black olives,
  chopped
1/4 cup capers, drained
1 1/2 pounds capellini

In a large saucepan heat the olive oil and sauté the garlic until lightly brown around the edges. Remove from heat. Add the anchovies and stir until they dissolve. Add the tomatoes, basil leaves and salt and pepper. Bring to a boil, lower heat and simmer for approximately 1 1/2 hours.

In a large saucepan heat half of the vegetable oil and sauté half of the eggplant over medium high heat until eggplant starts to soften and brown. Drain on paper towels. Repeat with remaining oil and eggplant.

Add the eggplant, olives and capers to the tomato sauce and cook until eggplant is very soft, about 30 to 45 minutes.

Cook capellini in lightly salted water, al dente. Drain and return pasta to the saucepan it was cooked in. Quickly pour in half of the tomato sauce and toss. Transfer pasta to a large serving bowl and pour remaining tomato sauce over top.

6 servings

Capellini with Pesto Sauce

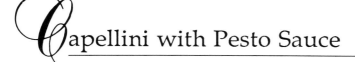

1 pound capellini

Cook capellini in lightly salted water, al dente. Drain well. Toss with the Pesto Sauce.

Pesto Sauce

1 3/4 cups basil leaves, well packed	1/4 teaspoon salt
	1/4 teaspoon pepper
1/4 cup pine nuts	4 ounces grated Parmesan cheese
2 cloves garlic	3/4 cup olive oil (approximately)

In a food processor puree the basil with the pine nuts, garlic, salt and pepper. Add the Parmesan cheese and about half of the oil. Mix well. Add more oil in a steady stream until it is absorbed and the sauce is smooth and creamy.

Dill Pesto Sauce: Follow the same directions but substitute with 2/3 cup fresh dill and 2/3 cup fresh parsley for the basil and 1/2 cup walnuts for the pine nuts.

4 to 6 servings

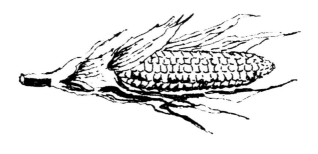

Tortellini and Artichoke Salad

1 pound frozen cheese-filled
  tortellini, cooked according to
  package directions
1 pint cherry tomatoes – halved
1/2 red onion, chopped
1 small red pepper, chopped
a 10-ounce package frozen petit
  peas, thawed

2 cups cooked broccoli florets
a 14-ounce can artichoke hearts,
  packed in water, drained and
  cut in quarters
a 6-ounce can pitted black olives,
  drained – sliced
chopped fresh parsley and dill
  for garnish

In a large bowl gently toss all the ingredients with the Dressing.
Garnish with parsley and dill.

8 to 10 servings

Dressing
1/4 cup milk
1/2 cup sour cream   +dill
1 1/2 cups mayonnaise
2 teaspoons bouillon powder

dash of red wine vinegar
1 teaspoon salt
pepper to taste

In a small bowl whisk together all the ingredients.

Feta Cheese and Pasta Salad

1 pound mixed (red, green, white)
  small pasta shells
1/2 pound Feta cheese, crumbled
2 large tomatoes, coarsely
  chopped
1 cup pitted black olives, coarsely
  chopped

1/4 cup chopped fresh parsley
1/4 cup pine nuts
1/3 cup olive oil
3 tablespoons lemon juice
1 clove garlic, crushed
1/2 teaspoon Tabasco sauce
salt and pepper to taste

Must be made in advance.

Cook pasta in lightly salted water, al dente. Drain well.
  Transfer pasta to a large bowl. Add the feta cheese, tomatoes,
olives, parsley and pine nuts and toss lightly.

In a small bowl combine the olive oil, lemon juice, garlic, Tabasco sauce and salt and pepper. Combine with the pasta.

Cover and refrigerate one to two hours or overnight.

Before serving, adjust the seasoning. If salad needs more marinade, mix olive oil and lemon juice in the same proportions and add to the pasta

Can be doubled or tripled.

4 to 6 servings

ℱusilli in Sun-Dried Tomato Sauce

1 pound fusilli
1/4 cups oil from sun-dried
   tomatoes
4 tablespoons (1/2 stick) unsalted
   butter
1 large onion, chopped
1 cup chopped celery
1 cup chopped carrots

3 cloves garlic
1 teaspoon fennel seeds
3/4 cup chopped sun-dried
   tomatoes
two 28-ounce cans Italian
   tomatoes, with juice
1 cup white wine
salt and pepper to taste

Cook the fusilli in lightly salted boiling water, al dente.

In a saucepan heat the oil and butter. Sauté the onion, celery, carrots, garlic and fennel seeds until vegetables are softened, about 15 minutes.

Stir in the sun-dried tomatoes, canned tomatoes, wine and salt and pepper. Simmer, uncovered, for 45 minutes, stirring occasionally.

Transfer the sauce to a food processor and mix until blended. Do not puree.

4 to 6 servings

Vermicelli and Mushroom Salad

8 ounces vermicelli, broken into
  pieces
a 6-ounce jar marinated artichoke
  hearts, drained and chopped
1 cup fresh mushrooms, sliced

3 tomatoes, sliced
1/2 cup chopped walnuts
2 tablespoons chopped fresh
  parsley

Cook vermicelli in lightly salted water, al dente. Drain well and pat dry with paper towels. Transfer to a bowl and toss a third cup of the Dressing with the vermicelli. Cover and refrigerate.

In a separate bowl toss remaining Dressing with the artichoke hearts and mushrooms. Cover and refrigerate.

Before serving, combine the pasta and mushroom mixture with the tomatoes, walnuts and parsley.

Dressing
1/4 cup vegetable oil
1/4 cup walnut oil  *or olive? or vinyard*
1/4 cup red wine vinegar

1 large clove garlic, minced
2 tablespoons chopped fresh basil
salt and pepper to taste

In a small bowl combine the oils, vinegar, garlic, basil and salt and pepper.

6 servings

Vegetable Lasagne

1 pound fresh spinach
1 tablespoon olive oil
5 ounces fresh mushrooms, sliced
1 cup grated carrot
1/2 cup chopped onion
a 15-ounce can tomato sauce
a 6-ounce can tomato paste

1/2 cup chopped pitted black
  olives
1 1/2 teaspoons dried oregano
6 ounces *fresh* lasagne noodles,
  uncooked
1 pound ricotta cheese
1 pound Monterey Jack cheese,
  sliced

Preheat oven to 375°.

Rinse spinach well. Tear into pieces and place in saucepan with just water clinging to the leaves and cook 3 to 4 minutes, stirring occasionally, until wilted. Squeeze dry.

In a saucepan heat the oil and sauté the mushrooms, carrot and onion until just tender. Stir in the tomato sauce, tomato paste, olives and oregano.

In a lasagne pan, layer half each of the noodles, ricotta cheese, spinach, Monterey Jack cheese and mushroom mixture. Repeat layers, reserving a few slices of Monterey Jack cheese for the top.

Bake for 30 minutes or until bubbling around edges. Let stand 10 minutes before cutting.

Can be made a day in advance. Recipe may be doubled or tripled.

Can be frozen. Bake, frozen, uncovered, at 350°, 45 to 60 minutes.

8 servings

Baked Chicken with Fettucine

1 pound fettucine	6 tablespoons dry sherry
1 cup (2 sticks) unsalted butter	1 cup grated Swiss cheese
4 tablespoons grated onion	1/2 pound fresh mushrooms,
4 tablespoons flour	sliced
4 cups chicken broth	4 cups cooked chicken breasts, cut *approx 4-½ breasts*
2 teaspoons salt	into bite-size pieces
1/2 teaspoon white pepper	1 cup grated Parmesan cheese
2 cups half and half	2/3 cup sliced almonds

Preheat oven to 350°. Butter a 11x13-inch baking dish.

very Large Cook fettucine in lightly salted water, al dente.

In a saucepan melt 1/2 cup of the butter and sauté the onion 5 minutes. Blend in the flour. Gradually add the broth, stirring constantly. Bring to a boil, lower heat and mix in the salt, pepper, half and half, sherry and Swiss cheese. Cook over low heat, stirring frequently, for 10 minutes. Adjust seasoning with salt and pepper.

Meanwhile, in another saucepan melt the remaining butter and sauté the mushrooms, stirring frequently, for 5 minutes.

Combine the sauce, mushrooms, fettucine, and chicken and place in the baking dish. Sprinkle with the Parmesan cheese and almonds. Bake for 30 minutes.

8 servings

×2

$\mathcal{H}$alf-Moon Pasta with Red Pepper Sauce

1 package won ton wrappers   Cheese Filling

Cut won ton wrappers into 3-inch rounds. Place 1/2 tablespoon of the Cheese Filling in center of each round. Moisten edges with water. Fold dough over filling, pressing edges to seal. Bend edges to form half-moon shapes. Arrange pasta on baking sheets.

Cheese Filling

7 ounces Montrachet cheese,
  softened
5 ounces St. André cheese, softened
a 3-ounce package cream cheese,
  softened

1/2 teaspoon dried rosemary,
  crumbled
4 tablespoons chopped fresh
  parsley

In a mixing bowl combine the cheeses, rosemary and parsley.

Cook pasta in lightly salted simmering water for about 1 minute. Pasta will rise to the surface when done. Drain well on paper towels and keep warm. Serve with Red Pepper Sauce.

Red Pepper Sauce

2 tablespoons unsalted butter
1/2 cup chopped onion
4 red peppers, cored, seeded and
  coarsely chopped (about 2 1/2
  cups)

dash of saffron
salt and pepper to taste
1/2 cup chicken broth
1/2 cup heavy cream

In a saucepan melt the butter and sauté the onion until soft. Add the red pepper, saffron and salt and pepper. Stir in the chicken broth. Bring liquid to a boil, cover and simmer for 10 minutes. Add the cream, stir and return to a boil. Pour mixture into a blender and puree. Keep warm.

4 servings

Bread *and* Muffins

Cheddar Cheese Bread

1 1/2 cups milk, scalded
2 tablespoons sugar
1 tablespoon salt
4 tablespoons (1/2 stick) unsalted
  butter
1 teaspoon dried oregano
6 cups flour, approximately

8 ounces sharp Cheddar cheese,
  grated
1 cup lukewarm water
3 packages dry yeast
1 egg white, lightly beaten
1 teaspoon water

In a large bowl combine the milk, sugar, salt, butter and oregano. Cool to lukewarm. Blend in 2 cups of the flour. Beat until smooth. Stir in the cheese.

In a large, warm bowl add the water and sprinkle in the yeast. Stir to dissolve. Blend in the milk mixture. Add enough of the remaining flour to make a soft dough. Knead the dough on a lightly floured board for almost 10 minutes until smooth and elastic.

Place in a buttered bowl, turning to coat the dough. Cover and let rise in a warm place, free from draft, until doubled in bulk, about 45 minutes.

Punch dough down. Turn out onto a lightly floured board and knead gently for 1 or 2 minutes. Halve dough. Shape into balls and place into 2 buttered 9x5-inch loaf pans. Cover and let rise again for about 30 minutes, until doubled in bulk.

Preheat oven to 375°.

Brush loaves with egg white mixed with water. Bake until dark golden brown, about 30 to 40 minutes. Loaves should sound hollow when tapped on the bottom.

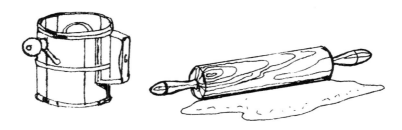

$\mathcal{S}$piral Herb Bread

3 cups flour
1 teaspoon salt
1 tablespoon unsalted butter
1 package dry yeast

1 cup very warm tap water (120° to 130°)
corn or vegetable oil
Herb Filling

In a food processor combine 2 cups of the flour, salt, butter and yeast. Process until butter is thoroughly cut into dry ingredients. Add half the water and turn the processor on and off 2 times. Add the remaining flour and water and let the processor run until a ball of dough forms on the blades. If the dough is too sticky add more flour, a tablespoon at a time. When correct consistency, let processor run 40 to 60 seconds to knead dough.

Turn dough out onto a lightly floured board and knead several times to form a smooth ball. Cover with plastic wrap and let rest for 20 minutes.

Oil a 9x5-inch loaf pan. Roll out the dough into a 9x12-inch rectangle, about 1/4 inch thick.

Spoon half the Filling on top and spread it over, leaving a margin of about one inch all around. Roll jelly-roll fashion and pinch the edges to seal. Place the filled dough in the prepared pan, seam side down.

Brush the top of the loaf with a little oil. Cover and let stand in a warm place for 50 to 60 minutes until slightly higher in the middle than around the edges.

Preheat oven to 375°.

Set the pan in the oven and bake about one hour. Cool on a wire rack.

Herb Filling
2 tablespoons unsalted butter
1 teaspoon finely minced garlic
3/4 cup finely chopped fresh
  parsley

3/4 cup finely chopped scallions
1/2 cup finely chopped fresh dill
salt and pepper to taste
1 teaspoon corn or peanut oil

In a saucepan melt the butter and add the garlic, parsley, scallions, dill and salt and pepper. Cook briefly.

AN ELEGANT DINNER PARTY

Westport enjoys a reputation for fine dining, both in its numerous restaurants and in the homes of gracious entertainers. No one has helped the town earn that reputation more than Martha Stewart, whose trend-setting recipes and entertaining guides have influenced the way America cooks. This talented writer, editor, cook, and businesswoman has also given her time and opened her home for many charitable organizations. The Stewart's home in Westport contains gardens where they grow much of the produce that the family uses and that Martha Stewart uses in her books and catering. This photograph was taken in the Stewart's home, and shows some of the elegant ideas that can be found in Martha Stewart's books.

 Onion and Black Pepper Flatbread

1 1/2 cups chopped onion
3 tablespoons olive oil plus 4
   teaspoons additional for
   drizzling the dough
3 cups flour
1 package dry yeast
1 tablespoon unsalted butter

1 cup very warm water
1 teaspoon salt
1 teaspoon coarsely ground pepper
   plus additional for sprinkling
   the dough
1/2 teaspoon kosher salt or to
   taste

Preheat oven to 500°. Oil two baking sheets.

In a saucepan, heat 3 tablespoons of the oil and sauté 1 cup of the onion until golden.

In a food processor combine 2 cups of the flour, yeast, and salt and butter. Process until the butter is thoroughly cut into dry ingredients. With the motor running add the remaining flour and water. Stop machine and add the pepper and the cooked onion. Blend the dough until it forms a ball adding more flour, if necessary, 1 tablespoon at a time.

Transfer the dough to a lightly floured surface and knead it for 15 seconds. Quarter the dough, form each piece into a 7x1/4-inch-thick round, and place the rounds on the baking sheets. With the finger, press indentations firmly into the dough at 2-inch intervals, drizzle the dough with the additional 4 teaspoons oil and sprinkle with the remaining 1/2 cup onion, the additional pepper and the kosher salt.

Bake the bread until it is golden, about 15 to 18 minutes.

Honey Spice Bread

1 package dry yeast
1/4 cup lukewarm water
1 egg
1/2 cup honey
1 tablespoon ground coriander
1/2 teaspoon ground cinnamon

1/4 teaspoon ground cloves
1 1/2 teaspoons salt
1 cup lukewarm milk
6 tablespoons (3/4 stick) unsalted
  butter, melted
4-4 1/2 cups flour

Butter two 9x5-inch loaf pans.

In a small bowl sprinkle the yeast over the lukewarm water and stir to dissolve.

In a large bowl combine the egg, honey, coriander, cinnamon, cloves and salt and whisk until well combined. Beat in the yeast mixture, milk and butter. Stir in the flour, 1/2 cup at a time until the dough can be gathered into a soft ball. Blend in remaining flour with the fingers.

Turn the dough out onto a lightly floured surface and knead until smooth and elastic. Do not add additional flour.

Form dough into a ball and place in a lightly buttered bowl, turning to coat. Cover and let rise until doubled in bulk.

Punch dough down and knead a few minutes. Divide in half and place in prepared pans. Let rise again until it almost reaches the top.

Preheat oven to 300°.

Bake until top is crusty and golden, about one hour. Cool on a wire rack.

hocolate Bread

2 cups flour
1 1/2 cups sugar
1 teaspoon baking soda
1/4 teaspoon cinnamon
1 cup (2 sticks) unsalted butter
3 1/2 tablespoons cocoa

1/2 cup water
2 eggs, beaten
1/2 cup buttermilk
1 teaspoon vanilla
2/3 cup chopped walnuts

Preheat oven to 350°. Butter a 9x5-inch loaf pan.

In a bowl combine the flour, sugar, baking soda and cinnamon.
In a saucepan mix the butter, cocoa and water and bring to a boil. When butter is melted, combine with flour mixture and mix until well moistened. Add the eggs, buttermilk and vanilla and blend well. Fold in the walnuts.
Pour into prepared pan and bake for one hour. Cool bread in pan on a wire rack.

ineapple-Zucchini Bread

3 eggs
1 cup oil
2 cups sugar
2 teaspoons vanilla
2 cups shredded zucchini
an 8-ounce can crushed pineapple,
    drained

3 cups flour
2 teaspoons baking soda
1/4 teaspoon baking powder
1 1/2 teaspoons cinnamon
3/4 teaspoon nutmeg
1 cup chopped dates
1 cup chopped pecans

Preheat oven to 350°. Butter two 9x5-inch loaf pans.

In a bowl combine flour, baking soda, baking powder, cinnamon and nutmeg.
In a mixer bowl beat the eggs, oil, sugar and vanilla until thickened. Add the zucchini and pineapple. Stir flour mixture into zucchini mixture. Add the dates and pecans. Mix well. Pour into loaf pans and bake for one hour.
Let breads cool in the pans on a wire rack.

Lemon Bread

1/4 cup flour
1 1/2 teaspoons baking powder
3/4 teaspoon salt
1 1/2 cups sugar
8 tablespoons (1 stick) unsalted
   butter, melted

3 eggs
3/4 cup milk
grated rind of 2 lemons
Lemon Glaze

Preheat oven to 350°. Butter three 2 1/2x5-inch "baby" loaf pans.

In a bowl combine the flour, baking powder and salt. Set aside.
In a mixer bowl blend together the sugar and butter. Beat in the eggs, one at a time.
Combine with the flour mixture, alternating with the milk. Stir in the lemon rind. Pour batter into prepared pans and bake for 1 hour.
Remove breads from oven and while still hot, pierce tops in several places with a toothpick. Pour Lemon Glaze *slowly* over tops, stopping to allow it to sink into the breads. When breads have cooled at least one hour, remove from pans.

Lemon Glaze
3/4 cup sugar   5 tablespoons lemon juice

In a small saucepan dissolve the sugar in the lemon juice.

Carrot Muffins

2 cups flour
1 1/4 cups sugar
2 teaspoons baking soda
1 teaspoon baking powder
2 teaspoons cinnamon
1/2 teaspoon salt
2 cups grated carrot
1/2 cup golden raisins

1/2 cup shredded coconut
1/2 cup chopped walnuts
1 tart green apple, peeled, cored
   and grated
3 eggs
1 cup vegetable oil
2 teaspoons vanilla

Preheat oven to 350°. Line 12 muffin tins with paper liners.

In a large mixing bowl combine the flour, sugar, baking soda, baking powder, cinnamon and salt. Stir in the carrot, raisins, coconut, walnuts and apple.

In a separate bowl beat the eggs, oil and vanilla with a wire whisk. Stir the egg mixture into the flour mixture, until batter is just combined.

Spoon into muffin tins. Fill to the top. Bake for 20 minutes.

Nutmeg Muffins

2 cups flour
1 1/2 cups packed brown sugar
12 tablespoons (1 1/2 sticks)
   unsalted butter
1 cup flour
2 teaspoons baking powder

2 teaspoons nutmeg
1/2 teaspoon baking soda
1/2 teaspoon salt
1 cup buttermilk
2 eggs, slightly beaten

Preheat oven to 350°. Line 24 muffin tins with paper liners.

In a bowl combine the 2 cups flour and brown sugar. Cut in the butter until mixture resembles coarse cornmeal. Reserve 1 cup for topping.

Add the 1 cup flour mixture, baking powder, nutmeg, baking soda and salt. Add the buttermilk and eggs. Stir just until moistened.

Spoon into muffin tins, filling one-half full. Sprinkle with the reserved flour mixture.

Bake until a cake tester inserted into the center comes out clean, about 20 minutes.

Remove from pans and let cool.

Orange Bran Muffins

2 1/2 cups flour
1/4 teaspoon salt
1 tablespoon baking soda
1 teaspoon baking powder
3 cups Raisin Bran cereal
1 cup sugar
1 teaspoon cinnamon

grated rind of 2 oranges
2 cups plain yogurt
2 eggs, beaten
1/4 cup vegetable oil
2 tablespoons sugar
1/2 teaspoon cinnamon

Preheat oven to 350°. Line 18 muffin tins with paper liners.

In a large bowl mix the flour, salt, baking soda and baking powder. Add the Raisin Bran, sugar, cinnamon and orange rind and mix well. Stir in the yogurt, eggs and oil.

Fill muffin tins full. Combine the sugar and cinnamon and sprinkle on top. Bake for 20 minutes.

Oatmeal Raisin Muffins

1 cup old-fashioned oats
1 cup raisins
1 cup boiling water
1 1/2 cups flour
2 teaspoons cinnamon
1 teaspoon baking powder
1 teaspoon baking soda
1 teaspoon salt

1 cup (2 sticks) unsalted butter,
   softened
1 cup brown sugar
1 cup sugar
2 eggs
1 teaspoon vanilla
1 cup chopped walnuts
1 cup flaked coconut

Preheat oven to 350°. Line 30 muffin tins with paper liners.

In a bowl mix the oats and raisins and pour the boiling water over all. Let stand 30 minutes.

In another bowl mix together the flour, cinnamon, baking powder, baking soda and salt. Set aside.

In a mixer bowl cream the butter with the sugars until fluffy. Beat in the eggs, one at a time. Add the vanilla. Stir in the flour mixture, oats, raisins, walnuts and coconut.

Spoon into muffin tins. Bake until cake tester inserted into the center comes out clean, about 20 to 25 minutes.

Remove from pans and let cool.

pple Muffins

2 cups flour
4 teaspoons cinnamon
1 teaspoon baking soda
1 teaspoon baking powder
6 tablespoons (3/4 stick) unsalted
  butter, softened
1/4 cup brown sugar

1/2 cup sugar
1 egg
1 cup buttermilk
2 large red apples, peeled and cut
  into 1/2-inch chunks
1/3 cup brown sugar

Preheat oven to 400°. Line 12 muffin tins with paper liners.

In a bowl mix the flour, cinnamon, baking soda and baking powder.

In a mixer bowl cream the butter and sugars until fluffy. Mix in the egg and quickly fold in the buttermilk. Do not overmix or batter will curdle.

Gradually stir in the flour mixture, making sure there are no lumps, but mixing no more than necessary. Fold in the apples.

Fill each muffin tin nearly to the top. Sprinkle the muffins with the 1/3 cup brown sugar.

Bake for 25 minutes. Open oven door and let stand in oven for 10 minutes.

lueberry Muffins

2 cups flour
1/2 teaspoon salt
2 teaspoons baking powder
6 tablespoons unsalted butter
1 1/2 cups plus 2 tablespoons sugar

2 eggs
1/2 cup milk
1 teaspoon vanilla
1 pint large blueberries, washed
  and dried well

Preheat oven to 375°. Butter *top* of muffin pan and line 12 muffin tins with paper liners.

In a bowl combine the flour, salt and baking powder.

In a mixer bowl cream the butter and 1 1/2 cups of the sugar. Add the eggs, one at a time. Add to the flour mixture, alternating with the milk in thirds. Add the vanilla.

Crush 1/2 cup of the blueberries with a fork and mix into the batter. Gently stir in the whole blueberries. Fill muffin tins up to the top. Sprinkle tops with the 2 tablespoons sugar. Bake for 30 minutes.

Turn off the heat and leave in the oven with door open, for 20 minutes.

Desserts

Chocolate Cinnamon Cake

8 tablespoons (1 stick) unsalted butter
1/2 cup vegetable oil
2 squares unsweetened chocolate
1 cup water
2 cups flour
1 teaspoon baking soda
2 cups sugar

1/2 cup sour milk (1 1/2 teaspoons vinegar plus milk to make 1/2 cup)
2 eggs, beaten
1 teaspoon cinnamon
1 teaspoon vanilla
Chocolate Frosting

Preheat oven to 350°. Butter and flour a 12x18-inch pan.

In a saucepan combine the butter, oil, chocolate and water and heat until chocolate is melted.

In a large bowl combine the flour, baking soda, sugar, milk, eggs, cinnamon and vanilla. Add the chocolate mixture and mix thoroughly. Pour batter into prepared pan. Bake 20 to 25 minutes. Five minutes before cake is done, prepare the Chocolate Frosting. *Frost the cake while it is still warm.*

Chocolate Frosting

8 tablespoons (1 stick) unsalted butter
2 squares unsweetened chocolate
6 tablespoons milk

a 1-pound box confectioners' sugar
1 teaspoon vanilla
1/2 cup chopped pecans

In a saucepan combine the butter, chocolate and milk. Heat until bubbles form around the edge. Remove from heat and beat in confectioners' sugar and vanilla. Add the pecans and mix well.

This recipe also makes 18 cupcakes. Fill muffin tins 3/4 full. Adjust baking time.

Chocolate Chocolate Cake

a 23-ounce package brownie mix
2 tablespoons water
3 eggs

whipped cream
Chocolate Filling
Chocolate Glaze

Preheat oven to 350°. Butter a 10x15-inch jelly-roll pan. Line with wax paper. Butter and flour wax paper. Butter a 2-quart charlotte mold.

In a mixer bowl beat together the brownie mix, water and eggs until smooth. Spread batter evenly in prepared pan and bake for 10 to 12 minutes. Remove from oven and cool slightly on a wire rack.

Gently peel paper away and cut cake rounds for the top and bottom and a strip to fit the sides of the charlotte mold.

Place smaller round in the bottom of the mold and wrap strip around the sides. Spoon Chocolate Filling into the mold. Top with second cake round. Chill until firm, about four hours.

Unmold cake and turn upside down. Spread with Chocolate Glaze on top and drizzle glaze down the sides of the cake. Chill. Serve with whipped cream.

Chocolate Filling
1 1/2 pounds semi-sweet chocolate
1/2 cup strong coffee, freshly
  brewed
3 eggs, separated

1/2 cup Tia Maria liqueur
3/4 cup sugar
1/2 cup heavy cream

In a double boiler melt the chocolate with the coffee. Remove from heat.

In a mixer bowl beat the egg yolks until pale yellow and stir into the chocolate. Stir in the Tia Maria liqueur and let cool.

In a separate bowl beat the egg whites, gradually adding the sugar, until stiff. Set aside.

In another bowl whip the cream and fold into the cooled chocolate mixture. Fold in the egg whites.

Chocolate Glaze
1/2 pound semi-sweet chocolate   1/3 cup water

Melt the chocolate with the water and stir until smooth.

Cake can be frozen. It can also be made in individual muffin molds.

pple Cake

3 cups flour
1 1/2 teaspoons baking soda
1/2 teaspoon salt
3 cups finely chopped apples,
   peeled
1/2 cup chopped walnuts

1 teaspoon grated lemon rind
1 cup sugar
1 1/2 cups vegetable oil
2 eggs
Cream Cheese Frosting
1 cup chopped walnuts

Preheat oven to 350°. Butter and flour three 9-inch round cake pans.

In a bowl combine the flour with the baking soda and salt.

In another bowl combine the apples, 1/2 cup chopped walnuts and lemon rind.

In a large mixing bowl combine the sugar, oil and eggs and beat well with a wooden spoon. Blend in the dry ingredients, mixing until smooth. Add the apple mixture and stir until well combined. Spread batter evenly into prepared pans.

Bake until surface springs back when pressed lightly, 30 to 40 minutes. Cool in pans for 10 minutes. Remove from pans and cool thoroughly on wire racks.

Fill and frost cake with Cream Cheese Frosting. Press remaining 1 cup walnuts onto sides.

Cream Cheese Frosting
an 8-ounce package cream cheese,
   softened
1 tablespoon unsalted butter,
   softened

1 tablespoon vanilla
1 pound confectioners' sugar

In a mixer bowl beat the cream cheese, butter and vanilla until light and creamy. Add the sugar and beat until of spreading consistency.

Kentucky Butter Cake

3 cups flour
1 teaspoon baking powder
1 teaspoon salt
1/2 teaspoon baking soda
1 cup (2 sticks) unsalted butter
2 cups sugar

4 eggs
1 cup buttermilk
2 teaspoons vanilla
Vanilla Sauce
confectioners' sugar or Mocha
    Frosting

Preheat oven to 325°. Butter and flour a 10-inch tube pan.

In a bowl combine the flour, baking powder, salt and baking soda. Set aside.

In a mixer bowl cream the butter and sugar well, gradually adding the eggs, one at a time and beating well after each addition.

Combine buttermilk and vanilla. Add alternately with dry ingredients to butter mixture, beginning and ending with dry ingredients. Blend well after each addition using low speed on electric mixer.

Pour into prepared pan. Bake until cake springs back when touched in center, about 60 minutes. Run spatula along edges of cake. Prick cake with a fork and pour *hot* Vanilla Sauce over the cake. Cool before removing from pan.

Before serving, sprinkle the cake with confectioners' sugar or frost with Mocha Frosting.

Vanilla Sauce
1 cup sugar
1/4 cup water

1/2 cup (1 stick) butter
1 teaspoon vanilla or almond
    extract

Heat sugar, water and butter until butter melts. Do not boil. Add the vanilla.

Mocha Frosting
8 tablespoons (1 stick) unsalted
    butter, softened
3 cups confectioners' sugar, sifted
1 egg yolk

2 ounces unsweetened chocolate
5 tablespoons strong coffee, freshly
    brewed
2 teaspoons vanilla or Cointreau

In a bowl cream the butter and sugar. Add the egg yolk. Dissolve the chocolate in the hot coffee. Cool and add to the butter mixture. Beat until creamy. Add the vanilla.

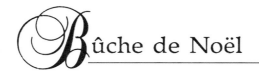

Bûche de Noël

Chocolate Sponge Cake

6 eggs, separated
3/4 cup sugar
6 ounces semi-sweet chocolate,
  melted
2 tablespoons strong coffee
1 teaspoon vanilla

1/4 cup cocoa for dusting
Chocolate Butter Cream
Meringue Mushrooms
almonds and confectioners' sugar for
  decoration

Preheat oven to 375°. Butter a 10x15-inch jelly-roll pan and line with parchment paper. Butter paper, dust with flour and shake pan to remove excess flour.

In a bowl beat the egg whites to soft peaks. Gradually add the sugar and beat to stiff peaks.

In another bowl beat the egg yolks lightly. Stir in the melted chocolate, coffee and vanilla. Fold a quarter of the meringue into the chocolate mixture. Pour back over meringue and fold in gently but thoroughly. Pour into prepared pan. Bake for 10 minutes.

Reduce heat to 350° and bake 5 minutes longer. Test center for doneness. Cool in pan.

Cut a piece of parchment paper a little larger than the pan, sprinkle with cocoa and carefully turn cake out onto the paper.

Fill with Chocolate Butter Cream.

Chocolate Butter Cream

1 1/3 cups sugar
1/3 cup water
3 egg whites
1/4 teaspoon cream of tartar
12 ounces semi-sweet chocolate,
  melted

3 tablespoons strong coffee or rum
1 teaspoon vanilla
1 cup (2 sticks) unsalted butter,
  softened

In a small saucepan dissolve the sugar in water over high heat. Boil to a soft ball stage (238° using a candy thermometer).

Meanwhile in another bowl beat the egg whites until foamy. Add the cream of tartar and beat until stiff. While continuing to beat the egg whites, add the sugar syrup in a thin stream. Beat at high speed for 5 minutes. Reserve 1/2 cup of the meringue for the mushrooms.

Beat in the melted chocolate, coffee and vanilla into remaining meringue. Gradually beat in the butter. Chill to spreading consistency, about 1/2 hour.

Meringue Mushrooms

Preheat oven to 200°.

With a pastry bag pipe caps and stems onto parchment-lined baking sheet. Pipe stems up. Using a knife hollow a spot in each cap to allow stem to fit in. Bake for 50 minutes. Cool. Attach caps and stems with reserved butter cream. Dust tops with cocoa. Place on top and around the log.

To assemble:

Spread butter cream on cake about 1/4-inch thick and carefully roll up, starting at short end. Frost with remaining butter cream, reserving an eighth of a cup for attaching the mushrooms. Texture frosting with fork tines to resemble a log.

Grind almonds in a food processor and place on ends of log.

Sift confectioners' sugar over all to resemble snow.

pice Cake

1 cup sugar	1 teaspoon ground cloves
1 cup light brown sugar	2 cups whipping cream
3 eggs	2 tablespoons unsalted butter,
2 cups cake flour	melted
1 teaspoon baking soda	confectioners' sugar or Triple Sec
1 teaspoon cinnamon	Frosting

Preheat oven to 350°. Butter and flour an angel food pan.

In a bowl mix the sugars and set aside.

In a mixer bowl beat the eggs until fluffy. Add the sugar mixture and beat until combined.

In another bowl sift the flour, baking soda, cinnamon and cloves, *four* times.

Gradually add the dry ingredients to the egg mixture alternating with the cream at low speed. Add butter and beat until smooth. Pour into prepared pan. Bake 35 minutes. Remove to wire rack and cool cake in pan.

Dust with confectioners' sugar before serving or frost with Triple Sec Frosting.

Triple Sec Frosting

2 cups confectioners' sugar	2 tablespoons Triple Sec
5 tablespoons unsalted butter, cut	1 tablespoon sour cream
into pieces, softened	pinch of salt

Place all ingredients in a food processor and mix until smooth.

heesecake

four 8-ounce packages of cream
   cheese, softened and cut into
   pieces
4 eggs
2 teaspoons vanilla

1 1/2 cups sugar
4 rounded tablespoons of flour
2 cups sour cream
3/4 cup milk
Graham Cracker Crust

Preheat oven to 350°.

In a food processor cream together 1 package of cream cheese and 1 egg. Repeat until all the cream cheese and eggs are blended. Add the vanilla, sugar and flour and mix thoroughly. Add the sour cream and milk and combine well. (If the processor bowl is a small one, transfer the mixture to a bowl and whisk in the sour cream and milk.)

Pour into prepared crust and bake for 45 minutes. Place a sheet of foil under pan to catch any drippings. Open oven door and continue baking for 15 minutes longer. Turn oven heat off and leave cake in the oven for 10 minutes. Cool on a wire rack.

Graham Cracker Crust
20 to 24 graham crackers
1 cup (2 sticks) butter, cut into pieces

2/3 cup confectioners' sugar

In a food processor crumble the graham crackers and process until crackers become fine crumbs. Add the butter and sugar and turn on and off several times until the butter is absorbed into the mixture.

Pat the cracker mixture evenly onto the bottom and sides of a 10-inch springform pan. Chill until ready to use.

To make Chocolate Marble Cheesecake:
a 6-ounce package semi-sweet chocolate chips   1/2 cup sugar

In the top of a double boiler melt the chocolate with the sugar. Remove from heat. Combine with a quarter of the cake batter. Swirl into cake.

Orange Nut Cake

1/2 cup almonds, toasted
1 cup farina
1 cup flour
1 teaspoon baking soda
2 tablespoons baking powder
grated rind of 1 orange
7 eggs, separated

1 cup (2 sticks) salted butter,
  softened
3/4 cup sugar
1/2 cup freshly squeezed orange
  juice
3 tablespoons Grand Marnier
Lemon Syrup
whipped cream (optional)

Preheat oven to 350°. Butter and flour a 10x14-inch baking pan.

Finely grind the almonds in a food processor. Set aside.

In a bowl combine the farina, flour, baking soda, baking powder and orange rind. Set aside.

In mixer bowl beat the egg whites until stiff. Set aside.

In a large bowl cream the butter, egg yolks and sugar until pale yellow. Gradually blend in half the flour mixture. Add the orange juice and Grand Marnier. Add remaining flour mixture. When thoroughly mixed, gently fold in the egg whites. Stir in the almonds.

Spread batter evenly into prepared pan. Bake until top is golden and a tester inserted in center comes out clean, about 35 minutes. Place on a wire rack and cool in pan. Pour Lemon Syrup on top.

Do not prepare the syrup until the cake has cooled.

Lemon Syrup
2 cups sugar
2 cups water

2 lemon or orange slices (necessary to
  prevent sugar from crystallizing)

In a small saucepan combine the sugar, water and lemon slices. Bring to a boil and boil hard for 8 minutes.

Remove from heat, discard lemon slices and immediately pour *hot* syrup slowly over cooled cake. Cover pan with foil and allow cake to sit until all the syrup is absorbed.

Cut into diamond-shape pieces by first removing crust all around the cake while still in the pan. Then cut lengthwise strips about 1 1/2 inches wide. Cut diagonally across the strips.

Serve with whipped cream sweetened to taste, if desired.

DINING AT THE HUNT CLUB

While Westport is hardly a town that time has forgotten, many vestiges of a simpler, quieter time do remain. One such place is the Fairfield County Hunt Club, whose members enjoy riding throughout the year. Westporters can often be found parked alongside the Club simply watching as riders jump their horses in competitions. For Westport, the Hunt Club is one of those cherished open spaces the town is fortunate to enjoy.

Praline Roll

Preheat oven to 350°. Butter a 12x18-inch jelly-roll pan. Line with parchment paper cut long enough to extend over edges. Butter paper and dust with flour, shaking out excess.

5 eggs, separated	1 scant tablespoon baking powder
3/4 cup sugar	confectioners' sugar
2 tablespoons warm water	Butter Cream Filling
1/2 cup flour	Praline Powder
1 1/2 tablespoons cornstarch	

Must be prepared a day in advance.

In a mixer bowl beat egg yolks until pale yellow. Gradually add the sugar, beating continuously until mixture forms a ribbon, about 5 minutes. Blend in water. Set aside.

In a bowl combine the flour, cornstarch and baking powder.

In another bowl beat the egg whites until stiff peaks form. Stir a quarter of the whites into the yolk mixture. Fold in the remaining whites. Sift dry ingredients over batter. Fold to blend thoroughly. Spread evenly into prepared pan. Bake until top of cake springs back when touched, about 12 to 15 minutes.

Dust top of cake lightly with sugar. Cover with damp towel and let cool, about 15 minutes.

Lightly dust two long, overlapping sheets of wax paper with the sugar. Turn cake out onto wax paper and let cool.

Butter Cream Filling

1 cup sugar	1 1/2 cups (3 sticks) butter, softened
5 tablespoons water	1 1/2 teaspoons vanilla
3 egg yolks	1 1/2 cups Praline Powder
2 eggs	

In a small saucepan combine the sugar and water. Set over medium-low heat and stir until sugar is dissolved. Cover and continue cooking until syrup registers 238° (soft-ball stage) on candy thermometer.

In a large mixing bowl combine the yolks and eggs and beat until mixture is thickened and forms a ribbon, about 5 minutes. When syrup is ready, gradually drizzle into eggs, beating constantly until all the syrup is absorbed. Continue beating until mixture has cooled to room temperature.

Gradually beat in the butter, 2 tablespoons at a time, making sure each piece is completely blended before adding another piece. The butter cream may separate toward the end but the last few pieces of butter will bring it back together into a smooth cream. Add vanilla and 1 1/2 cups Praline Powder and blend well. *Can be made 2 days in advance.*

To assemble:

Spread half of the butter cream over top of cake. Gently roll up and transfer to serving platter. Spread remaining butter cream over entire surface of roll. Refrigerate.

Let stand at room temperature one hour before serving.

Praline Powder

2 cups sugar	1/4 teaspoon cream of tartar
2/3 cup water	2 cups whole almonds

Generously oil a 12x18-inch jelly-roll pan.

In a heavy saucepan combine the sugar, water and cream of tartar. Cook over low heat stirring frequently until the sugar is dissolved, washing down any crystals that form on sides of pan with small pastry brush dipped repeatedly in warm water. Cover and continue cooking 1 minute to dissolve any remaining crystals.

Add the almonds and cook, without stirring, until almonds are browned and syrup has caramelized, about 5 to 7 minutes. The mixture is ready when almonds start cracking and caramel bubbles become larger and slower.

Immediately pour syrup onto prepared pan. Let cool several minutes. Break the brittle into pieces and grind in a food processor.

Cake can be made up to three days in advance and refrigerated.

10 to 12 servings

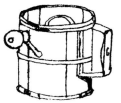

alnut Torte

8 eggs, separated
5 egg whites
1 cup sugar
1 pound walnuts, finely ground

2 tablespoons fresh bread crumbs
1 teaspoon baking powder
Butter Frosting

Best made one day ahead.   Store in refrigerator.

Preheat oven to 350°. Butter two 9-inch round pans. Line with wax paper. Butter paper and dust with flour.

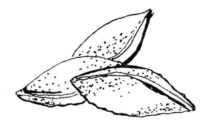

In a mixer bowl beat the egg yolks with sugar until pale yellow. Add the walnuts, bread crumbs and baking powder.

In another bowl beat the egg whites until stiff. Fold into walnut mixture.

Pour into prepared pans and bake 40 to 45 minutes. Let cool.

Butter Frosting
5 egg yolks
5 tablespoons sugar
5 tablespoons milk

2 teaspoons powdered coffee
1 cup (2 sticks) unsalted butter,
   softened

In a blender mix the egg yolks and sugar. Add the milk, coffee and butter.

To assemble:
Spread about a third of the Butter Frosting over the bottom layer. Cover with top layer and spread remaining frosting over top and sides of the cake.

Pumpkin Roll

2/3 cup canned pumpkin
1 cup sugar
1 teaspoon lemon juice
3/4 cup flour
1 teaspoon baking powder
2 teaspoons cinnamon
1 teaspoon ginger

1/2 teaspoon nutmeg
1/2 teaspoon salt
3 eggs
1 cup finely chopped walnuts
1/4 cup confectioners' sugar
Cream Cheese Filling

Preheat oven to 375°. Butter a 10x15-inch jelly-roll pan. Line with parchment paper. Butter paper, dust with flour and shake pan to remove excess.

In a bowl mix together the pumpkin, sugar, lemon juice, flour, baking powder, cinnamon, ginger, nutmeg and salt.

In another bowl, beat the eggs for 5 minutes on high speed and fold into pumpkin mixture. Spread batter in prepared pan and top with walnuts.

Bake for 15 minutes. While still warm turn onto a towel sprinkled with confectioners' sugar. Starting at the narrow end, roll up with the towel and refrigerate about two hours.

Unroll pumpkin roll, carefully remove towel and spread with Cream Cheese Filling. Reroll and chill half an hour.

Cream Cheese Filling
1 cup confectioners' sugar
an 8-ounce package cream cheese,
  softened

4 tablespoons (1/2 stick) unsalted
  butter, softened
1/2 teaspoon vanilla

In a bowl combine all the ingredients.

estport Cake

1 yellow cake mix
1/2 cup (1 stick) unsalted butter,
  softened
2 eggs
1 teaspoon vanilla

an 8-ounce package cream cheese,
  softened
3 1/4 cups confectioners' sugar
2 eggs
1/2 cup chopped walnuts
confectioners' sugar

Preheat oven to 350°. Butter and flour a 9x13-inch pan.

Combine the cake mix, butter, the 2 eggs and vanilla by hand. (Do not use a mixer.) Mixture will be thick and crumbly. Press mixture firmly onto bottom and sides of prepared pan.

In a bowl combine the cream cheese, sugar and 2 eggs. Beat until smooth. Spread the cream cheese mixture over the crumb mixture. Sprinkle with walnuts. Bake about 35 to 40 minutes. Cool on a wire rack. Dust with confectioners' sugar. Cut into squares.

yllabub

pared rind of 1 lemon
4 tablespoons lemon juice
crushed pulp of 1/2 lemon
6 tablespoons sherry

3 tablespoons brandy
1/2-3/4 cup sugar
1 cup heavy cream
ground nutmeg

In a bowl combine the lemon rind, juice, pulp, sherry and brandy. Set aside for several hours.

Strain the lemon mixture into a large mixer bowl. Add the sugar and beat until dissolved. Slowly add the cream and beat until mixture forms peaks.

Spoon into four tall glasses and sprinkle with the nutmeg. Serve immediately.

Meringue Cake with Strawberries

4 egg whites
pinch of salt
1/4 teaspoon cream of tartar
1 cup sugar
6 ounces semi-sweet chocolate
  pieces

3 tablespoons water
3 cups heavy cream
1/3 cup sugar
1 pint strawberries, sliced, plus 5-8
  whole strawberries

Preheat oven to 250°. Line two baking sheets with wax paper and trace three 8-inch circles. Lightly butter the circles.

In a bowl beat together the egg whites with the salt and cream of tartar. Gradually add the sugar and continue beating until meringue is stiff and glossy.

Spread the meringue about 1/4-inch thick evenly over each circle. Bake 20 to 25 minutes until pale golden but still pliable. Remove from oven and carefully peel away the wax paper. Place on wire racks to dry.

In the top of a double boiler melt the chocolate with water. Set aside.

In a bowl whip the heavy cream. Gradually add the 1/3 cup sugar and beat until stiff.

Dip the whole strawberries in the chocolate and allow to dry.

To assemble:

Place meringue layer on serving plate and spread with a thin coat of melted chocolate. Then spread a 3/4-inch thick layer of whipped cream and top with half of the sliced strawberries. Repeat for second layer. Top with third meringue circle and frost sides with remaining whipped cream. Decorate top with remaining chocolate and whole strawberries.

Chill for at least two hours.

Recipe may be doubled and even quadrupled. Use a trifle bowl for a large quantity.

8 servings

239

Orange Marmalade Soufflé with Grand Marnier Sauce

Butter the bowl and the inside lid of a 2-quart double boiler. Heat the water to the simmering point.

Soufflé

2/3 cup egg whites (about 6 egg whites), room temperature
1/4 teaspoon salt
4 tablespoons sugar

2 tablespoons orange marmalade
grated rind of 1 orange
Grand Marnier Sauce

In a large mixer bowl beat the egg whites with salt until soft peaks form. Add the sugar, 1 tablespoon at a time, and then add the marmalade, 1 tablespoon at a time, while beating continuously. Beat until just blended. Gently fold in the orange rind.

Spoon soufflé mixture into the double boiler, cover and steam one hour. *(Can be steamed up to two hours without harm.)*

Serve with Grand Marnier Sauce.

Grand Marnier Sauce

1 egg yolk
1 1/4 cup confectioners' sugar
3 to 4 tablespoons Grand Marnier

3/4 cup whipping cream, whipped to soft peaks

In a bowl beat the egg yolk until just blended. Add the sugar and Grand Marnier and beat with a whisk until smooth. Gently fold in the whipped cream. Spoon soufflé into four individual bowls. Spoon sauce over top.

Serve immediately.

Fruit Turnovers

1 cup (2 sticks) unsalted butter,
  softened
two 3-ounce packages cream cheese,
  softened
2 cups flour

1/2 teaspoon salt
a 12-ounce jar fruit preserves
  (apricot, peach, etc.)
1/2 cup chopped walnuts
confectioners' sugar

Preheat oven to 400°. Butter and flour a baking sheet.

In a bowl combine the butter and cream cheese with a spoon.
Blend in flour and salt and mix well. Refrigerate for one hour.
Remove from refrigerator and allow to stand for 30 minutes.
  On a lightly-floured surface roll out dough to 1/16-inch thick.
Cut circles with a 3-inch biscuit cutter. Combine the fruit
preserves with the walnuts. Spoon one rounded teaspoon of
preserve mixture on half of the circle. Fold dough over filling
and pinch edges together to seal well. Crimp with a fork.
  Bake for 8 to 10 minutes. Cool. Sprinkle with confectioners'
sugar.
  *Can be frozen and baked without thawing. Increase baking time
slightly.*

Chocolate Mousse

12 ounces semi-sweet chocolate
1/4 cup boiling water
8 eggs, separated

4-5 tablespoons Grand Marnier
dash of cream of tartar
whole strawberries

Chop chocolate in a processor. Add the water and blend for 25
seconds. Add the egg yolks and Grand Marnier and blend until
smooth. Cool slightly.
  In a mixer bowl beat the egg whites with cream of tartar until
stiff but not dry. Gently fold into chocolate mixture.
  Pour mousse into six serving glasses and chill at least 2 hours.
Before serving, place 2 to 3 strawberries on top.

Chocolate Mousse Pie

1 pound semi-sweet chocolate	6 tablespoons confectioners' sugar
2 eggs	Chocolate Wafer Crust
4 eggs, separated	Whipped Cream Topping
2 cups whipping cream	chocolate curls

In the top of a double boiler melt the chocolate. Let cool to lukewarm. Add the 2 eggs and mix well. Add the 4 egg yolks and mix until thoroughly blended.

In a mixer bowl whip the cream with the sugar until soft peaks form. In another bowl, beat the egg whites until stiff but not dry. Stir a little of the cream and whites into the chocolate mixture to lighten. Fold in the remaining cream and whites and combine well. Turn into prepared pan and chill thoroughly.

Before serving, top with Whipped Cream Topping and chocolate curls.

Chocolate Wafer Crust

1 1/2 boxes chocolate wafers, ground	1/2 cup (1 stick) unsalted butter, melted

In a bowl combine the crumbs and butter. Press on the bottom and completely up the sides of a 10-inch springform pan. Chill.

Whipped Cream Topping

2 cups whipping cream	confectioners' sugar

Whip the cream with the sugar to taste until quite stiff.

To assemble:

Carefully remove the springform. Spread whipped cream over top of filling. Shave chocolate with a vegetable peeler into curls and decorate top.

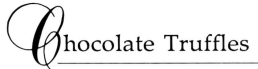

Chocolate Truffles

12 ounces dark sweet chocolate,
  chopped
4 large egg yolks, beaten lightly
1/4 cup heavy cream
10 tablespoons (1 1/4 sticks)
  unsalted butter, cut into pieces,
  softened

3 tablespoons bourbon or rum
1/2 teaspoon vanilla
1/3 cup Dutch process cocoa or 1/2
  cup finely chopped walnuts for
  coating the truffles

In the top of a double boiler melt the chocolate, stirring until it is smooth. Remove and set aside.

In a saucepan combine the egg yolks and the cream. Cook the mixture over low heat, stirring constantly, until it is thickened. Do not let it boil. Remove the saucepan from the heat and stir in the chocolate. Transfer to a bowl.

With an electric mixture beat in the butter and continue beating until the mixture is thick and smooth. Mix in the bourbon and vanilla. Cover and chill until firm, about 4 hours.

To make the truffles:
Line a jelly-roll pan with wax paper.

Scoop out a heaping teaspoon of the chocolate mixture, roll it into a ball and roll the ball in the cocoa, coating it completely.

Arrange the balls on the pan as they are made and chill them until they are firm, about two hours.

Transfer the truffles to an airtight container and keep chilled until ready to serve. The truffles will keep for up to three days.

50 truffles

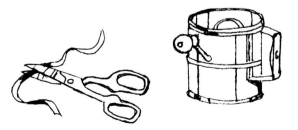

Mandarin Chocolate Sherbet

1 tablespoon unflavored gelatin
3 1/2 cups water
2 cups sugar
6 ounces semi-sweet chocolate,
  melted

1 cup fresh orange juice
1 teaspoon vanilla
2 tablespoons Cointreau liqueur

In a small bowl soften the gelatin in 1/2 cup of the water.

In a saucepan combine the remaining 3 cups of water and the sugar. Bring to a boil and boil for 5 minutes. Remove from heat and add the softened gelatin to hot syrup beating vigorously. Mix together the syrup and chocolate. Add the orange juice, vanilla and Cointreau.

Let cool completely.

Freeze mixture in ice cream maker according to manufacturer's directions.

1 1/2 quarts

Grand Marnier Coupe

4 cups fresh strawberries, sliced or
  raspberries
sugar

1 quart vanilla ice cream
Grand Marnier Topping

In a bowl lightly toss the strawberries with the sugar. Cover and refrigerate.

Grand Marnier Topping
5 egg yolks
1/2 cup plus 2 tablespoons sugar

1/2 cup Grand Marnier
1 cup heavy cream

In the top of a double boiler place the yolks and the 1/2 cup of sugar . Beat continuously until the yolks are pale yellow and very thick, about 10 minutes. Remove top from double boiler and stir in 1/4 cup of the Grand Marnier. Let cool. Cover and refrigerate.

In a bowl beat the heavy cream with the 2 tablespoons sugar until almost stiff. Fold into cold Grand Marnier sauce. Stir in the remaining liqueur.

To serve:
Place a scoop of ice cream into eight tall glasses. Top with some of the strawberries and cover with 3 to 4 tablespoons of the Grand Marnier Topping.

244

offee Ice Cream Pie

1/2 to 3/4 gallon vanilla ice cream, softened

2 1/2 cups chopped "Heath English Toffee" or "Skor" bars (14 -16)
Vanilla Wafer Crust

Spoon ice cream into Vanilla Wafer Crust. Sprinkle about 1/2 cup of chopped toffee bars and continue layering three more times, ending with the chopped toffee. Reserve 1/2 cup of the toffee for the sauce. Freeze pie.

Remove from freezer 5 to 10 minutes before serving. Serve with warmed Sauce.

Vanilla Wafer Crust
18 vanilla or brown edge wafers

Butter a 9-inch pie plate. Line the bottom and sides with wafers.

Sauce

1 1/2 cups sugar
1 cup evaporated milk
8 tablespoons (1 stick) unsalted butter

1/4 cup light corn syrup
dash of salt
1/2 cup reserved chopped toffee bars

In a saucepan combine all the ingredients except the chopped toffee bars. Bring to a boil over low heat and boil 1 minute. Remove from heat and stir in remaining chopped toffee. Cool slightly, stirring occasionally.

assis Ice Cream

2 cups black currant preserves
1 cup Crème de Cassis liqueur
juice of 1 lemon

1/2 teaspoon vanilla
2 cups light cream
2 cups heavy cream

In a food processor puree the preserves with a little of the Cassis liqueur. Add the lemon juice, the remaining Cassis and vanilla.

In a bowl mix the creams together. Stir in the Cassis mixture and combine until thoroughly mixed.

Freeze mixture in ice cream maker according to manufacturer's directions.

1 1/2 quarts

Pears with Raspberry Sauce

1 1/2 cups water
1 1/2 cups sugar

1/2 teaspoon vanilla
4 firm pears, peeled, halved and
cored

In a saucepan combine the water and sugar. Bring to a boil and boil 5 minutes. Lower heat, add the vanilla and pears and simmer until the fruit is just tender. Drain and chill the pears.

Raspberry Sauce
a 10-ounce package frozen
raspberries, thawed
1 tablespoon sugar
1 teaspoon cornstarch

2 tablespoons water
1 tablespoon Kirsch
blanched slivered almonds for
decoration

In a saucepan combine the raspberries with the sugar. Combine the cornstarch with the water and mix with the raspberries. Simmer until soft. Press raspberry mixture through a fine sieve to remove seeds. Add Kirsch and chill.

To assemble:
Place pears in a deep dish just large enough to hold the pears in one layer and spoon Raspberry Sauce over them. Sprinkle with the almonds.

Pears with Crème Anglaise

Poach pears as above and add 1 teaspoon fresh lemon juice, a dash of cinnamon and 2 cloves to the cooking ingredients.

Crème Anglaise
4 egg yolks
1/3 cup sugar
1 teaspoon cornstarch
1 1/4 cups scalded milk

1/2 cup heavy cream
1 tablespoon Grand Marnier or
Cointreau

In a mixer bowl beat the egg yolks with the sugar until eggs form a ribbon. Add the cornstarch. Slowly add the milk. Pour the cream in a steady stream. Transfer to a saucepan and cook over low heat, stirring continuously, until thickened. Remove from heat, add Grand Marnier and cool, stirring frequently.

Amaretto Cream Puffs with Raspberry Sauce

Puffs

1/2 cup water

4 tablespoons (1/2 stick) unsalted butter

1/2 cup flour

1 teaspoon sugar

2 large eggs

Preheat oven to 375°.

In a large saucepan heat the water and butter until water has come to a boil and butter melts. Lower heat and add the flour and sugar all at once. Stir briskly with a wooden spoon until mixture forms a ball and leaves the sides of the pan.

Remove from heat and cool slightly. Beat in the eggs, one at a time, until well combined.

Drop dough by heaping tablespoons onto *ungreased* baking sheet. Make 10 puffs. Bake until puffs are golden brown, about 30 to 35 minutes.

With a metal spatula transfer puffs to a wire rack and let cool 5 minutes. With the tip of a knife make holes on the bottom of the puffs and pipe in the Amaretto Filling. Serve with Raspberry Sauce.

Amaretto Filling

1 cup heavy cream

1 tablespoon plus 1 teaspoon sugar

1/4 cup Amaretto liqueur

Fit a pastry bag with a #1 tip. Set aside.

In a small bowl whip the cream and sugar until very stiff. Gently fold in the Amaretto liqueur. Spoon into pastry bag and pipe mixture into each puff through the hole on the bottom or spoon in the filling.

Can be made a day in advance up to this point.

Raspberry Sauce

two 10-ounce packages frozen raspberries in syrup, thawed

2 teaspoons cornstarch

1 tablespoon water

confectioners' sugar (optional)

Place the raspberries and syrup in a blender and puree for 10 seconds. In a small saucepan mix the cornstarch with the water. Add the raspberry puree and heat until the mixture starts to boil. Remove from heat and cool.

Recipe can be doubled.

Charlotte Russe

an 8-ounce package cream cheese,
  softened
1 cup sugar
1 pint whipping cream

1 teaspoon vanilla
Ladyfingers
Raspberry Topping

Must be prepared in advance.

Cut Ladyfingers in half. Line a 9-inch springform pan on sides and bottom with the Ladyfingers.

In a mixer bowl beat the cream cheese, sugar and vanilla until very creamy, almost fluffy.

In a separate bowl, whip the cream until it holds peaks. Gently fold the cream into the cheese mixture.

Spread half of the mixture into the prepared pan. Add a layer of Ladyfingers. Pour in remaining mixture. Cover and refrigerate overnight.

To assemble:
Unmold the cake and cut into slices. Top with the raspberries.

Ladyfingers
4 eggs, separated
1/2 cup sugar

1/2 teaspoon vanilla
2/3 cup flour

Preheat oven to 350°. Place wax paper on 2 cookie sheets.

In a bowl beat the egg yolks and sugar until very thick and pale yellow.

In a separate bowl beat the egg whites until very stiff. Take half of the egg whites and gently fold into the yolk mixture. Fold in the flour, a small amount at a time. Fold in the remaining egg whites. Using a pastry bag and a plain tube or with a spoon, form 4 1/2-inch long ladyfingers. Bake until lightly colored, about 10 to 15 minutes. Do not let them brown. *Can be made several days in advance.*

Raspberry Topping
two 10-ounce packages
  unsweetened frozen raspberries,
  thawed

1 tablespoon Kirsch liqueur

In a food processor blend the raspberries and Kirsch.

trawberry Tarts

1 1/2 cups flour
1 tablespoon sugar
1/4 teaspoon salt

6 tablespoons (3/4 stick) unsalted
   butter, cold
2 tablespoons shortening
4 tablespoons cold water

Preheat oven to 350°.

In a bowl combine the flour, sugar and salt. Cut in the butter and shortening. Toss with the water. Gather into a ball, divide into 6 parts, wrap each separately and refrigerate for 30 minutes.

Turn 6 aluminum 1/2-cup molds upside down. Roll out each piece of dough 1/8-inch thick and cover the *outside* of each mold. Trim excess dough and prick all over with a fork. Place dough side up on a baking sheet. Bake 10 to 12 minutes. Cool completely on the molds.

Remove shells from molds and set upright on a baking sheet. Fill with Melted Chocolate.

Reduce oven temperature to 200°.

Melted Chocolate
3 ounces semi-sweet chocolate, finely chopped

Sprinkle 1/2 ounce of chocolate on the bottom of each tart. Set in oven until the chocolate is soft. Remove the tarts and spread the chocolate evenly over the bottom of each shell. Cool 10 minutes. Divide Grand Marnier Filling among the tarts. Top with Strawberry Filling.

Grand Marnier Filling
an 8-ounce package cream cheese,
   softened
3 tablespoons sugar

1 tablespoon Grand Marnier
1/2 teaspoon vanilla
2 tablespoons heavy cream

In a bowl combine the cream cheese, sugar, Grand Marnier, vanilla and heavy cream.

Strawberry Topping
36 to 48 hulled whole
   strawberries
1/3 cup seedless raspberry jam,
   slightly warmed

whipped cream and confectioners'
   sugar (optional)

Toss the strawberries with the jam. Top each tart with 6 to 8 strawberries.

Serve with sweetened whipped cream, if desired.

A CHRISTMAS FEAST

DESSERT AND COFFEE

In its fundraising efforts, the League sponsors a variety of events, some like the annual Creative Arts Festival requiring monumental volunteer hours. Others, though smaller in scale, often give members a chance to display their individual talents. The Christmas tree in this photograph was one of those mini-fundraisers. League members donated tiny bears and made stenciled ornaments in workshops for the tree which was auctioned at a Christmas Tree Festival sponsored by a local nonprofit group. The winning bidder was, not surprisingly, a League member who felt it would be a perfect touch to complement her bear collection. Traditions run strong among League members. For example, the tea set and doll in this scene belong to a little girl whose League mother has been collecting them lovingly for years.

Country Plum Tart

2 pounds plums, quartered and
  pitted
1 cup sugar
1 tablespoon cornstarch
2 tablespoons water
2 1/4 cups flour
2 teaspoons baking powder
1/2 teaspoon baking soda

1/2 teaspoon salt
12 tablespoons (1 1/2 sticks)
  unsalted butter
1 1/2 cups sugar
2 eggs
1 teaspoon vanilla
1 cup sour cream

In a saucepan combine the plums with the sugar. Let stand until juices flow. Heat slowly until mixture begins to boil. Dissolve cornstarch in water and add to the plums. Stir together until thickened. Remove from heat, drain and reserve juice.

Preheat oven to 350°. Butter and flour a 9x13-inch pan.

Combine the flour, baking powder, baking soda and salt.
In a mixer bowl cream together the butter, sugar, eggs and vanilla. Add the dry ingredients to the butter mixture alternating with the sour cream and ending with the dry ingredients.
Spread half of the batter in the prepared pan. Sprinkle with half of the Walnut Topping. Add half of the drained plums. Spoon over rest of the batter to cover. Arrange the remaining plums, skin side down, over the batter. Sprinkle on the remaining topping. Drizzle half of the reserved plum juice over the plums.
Bake for 50 minutes. Add the remaining plum juice and bake 10 minutes longer. Remove and cool.

Walnut Topping
1/2 cup chopped walnuts
1 teaspoon cinnamon

2 tablespoons sugar

Combine all the ingredients.

Cranberry and Apple Tart

3/4 cup fresh cranberries
1/3 cup sugar
1/4 cup currants
1/4 cup cognac
1 teaspoon grated orange rind
1 cup sugar
2 tablespoons flour
1 teaspoon cornstarch

1/8 teaspoon nutmeg
8 tart green apples, peeled, cored
  and sliced
1 egg, beaten, combined with 1
  tablespoon milk
1 tablespoon sugar
1/8 teaspoon cinnamon
Pastry Dough

In a food processor chop the cranberries coarsely. Transfer to a bowl and mix with the 1/3 cup sugar. Let stand one hour.

Preheat oven to 425°.

In a small bowl combine the currants and cognac and set aside.
In a large bowl combine the orange rind with the 1 cup sugar, flour, cornstarch and nutmeg. Stir in the apples, cranberries and currants. Fill prepared tart pan and make Lattice Top.
Bake tart for 20 minutes. Reduce heat to 350° and bake 35 to 40 minutes longer.

Pastry Dough
pastry for 10-inch tart and for lattice top

Line tart pan with pastry and cut pastry strips for lattice top. Refrigerate until ready to use.

Lattice Top
Brush the pastry strips with the combined egg and milk. Arrange strips on top of the pie. Mix the 1 tablespoon sugar with the cinnamon and sprinkle over pie.

8 to 10 servings

evonshire Tart

pastry for 9-inch tart pan
rind of 1 lemon
5 tablespoons sugar
an 8-ounce package cream cheese,
   softened

1 tablespoon lemon juice
3 tablespoons heavy cream
fresh fruit (strawberries, kiwi,
   bananas, grapes)
Apricot Glaze

Preheat oven to 450°.

Line tart pan with pastry. Prick bottom with a fork. Bake crust until lightly browned, about 12 to 15 minutes. Cool completely on a wire rack.

In a food processor chop the lemon rind with the sugar. Add the cream cheese, lemon juice and heavy cream and combine well.

Spread filling mixture evenly into prepared crust. Cover filling with the fruit and brush with Apricot Glaze.

Refrigerate at least one hour.

Apricot Glaze
1/2 cup apricot preserves

In a small saucepan melt the apricot preserves over low heat. Press through a sieve set over a small bowl.

Food Processor Pie Crust

Double Crust	Single Crust
2 cups flour	1 cup flour
1 teaspoon salt	1/4 teaspoon salt
8 tablespoons (1 stick) frozen unsalted butter cut into quarters	4 tablespoons (1/2 stick) frozen unsalted butter cut into quarters

Place all the ingredients in a food processor and blend until dough is crumbly, about 15 seconds.

1/3 cup cold water	3 tablespoons cold water

While processor is running, add the water, all at once. Do not process more than 20 seconds. If dough has not formed a ball, shape with hands. Wrap in plastic wrap and chill dough half an hour.

Pâte Brisée: Omit the salt and add 1 tablespoon or. 1 teaspoon sugar.

Chocolate Date Squares

1/2 pound pitted dates, chopped	1/4 teaspoon salt
1 teaspoon baking soda	1 3/4 cups flour
1 cup boiling water	2 tablespoons cocoa
1 cup (2 sticks) unsalted butter	a 12-ounce package semi-sweet chocolate chips
1 cup sugar	1 1/2 cups chopped walnuts
2 eggs	
1 teaspoon vanilla	

Preheat oven to 350°. Butter and flour a 9x13-inch pan.

In a bowl sprinkle the baking soda over the dates. Add the water and set aside.

In another bowl beat the butter with the sugar, eggs, vanilla and salt until creamy.

Sift flour with cocoa and add to the butter mixture. Combine with the date mixture and pour into prepared pan. Top with chocolate chips and walnuts.

Bake about 35 minutes. Cool and cut into squares.

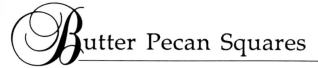

Butter Pecan Squares

1 1/2 cups flour
1/3 cup sugar

8 tablespoons (1 stick) unsalted
   butter, softened
1/2 teaspoon grated lemon rind

Preheat oven to 375°. Butter a 9-inch square baking pan.

In a mixer bowl combine all ingredients and beat at low speed until mixture resembles coarse meal. Press onto bottom of the prepared pan. Bake for 10 to 15 minutes or until edges are lightly browned. Pour Pecan Topping over partially baked pastry shell and bake until topping is set, about 20 to 25 minutes. Cut into squares when thoroughly cooled.

Pecan Topping
2/3 cup sugar
3/4 cup honey
2 eggs
2 tablespoons flour
1/4 teaspoon salt

1 1/2 teaspoons vanilla
2 tablespoons unsalted butter,
   melted
1 cup chopped pecans

Combine all the ingredients except the pecans. Mix at low speed until well blended, 1 to 2 minutes. Stir in the pecans.

24 squares

Lemon Bars

2 cups flour
4 tablespoons sugar
1/4 teaspoon salt
10 tablespoons (1 1/4 sticks)
   unsalted butter
3 eggs, beaten
1 cup dark brown sugar
3/4 cup chopped pecans

3/4 cup coconut
2 teaspoons vanilla
peeled rind of 2 lemons
2 1/4 cups confectioners' sugar
4 tablespoons lemon juice
2 tablespoons unsalted butter,
   softened

Preheat oven to 350°. Butter a 10x15-inch jelly-roll pan.

In a food processor mix together the flour, sugar, salt and butter until it resembles coarse meal. Press onto prepared pan and bake 10 to 15 minutes. Cool slightly.

In a bowl mix the eggs, brown sugar, pecans, coconut and vanilla and pour over partially baked pastry. Bake until topping is firm, about 20 to 30 minutes.

In the bowl of a food processor chop the lemon rind with the sugar. Add the lemon juice and butter and mix until smooth. Spread on top. Cut into squares when thoroughly cooled.

60 bars

# Date and Walnut Pinwheels

2 cups flour
1/2 teaspoon baking soda
12 tablespoons (1 1/2 sticks)
  unsalted butter, softened
1/2 cup sugar

1/2 cup dark brown sugar
1 egg
1 teaspoon vanilla
Date Walnut Filling

In a bowl combine the flour and baking soda. Set aside.

In a mixer bowl cream the butter with the sugars until light and fluffly. Beat in the egg and vanilla. At low speed, beat in the flour mixture just until combined. Divide dough in half. Wrap in plastic wrap and chill for one hour.

Date Walnut Filling
8 ounces chopped dates
3 tablespoons sugar
2 tablespoons lemon juice

1/3 cup water
1/4 cup chopped walnuts

In a small saucepan combine the dates, sugar, lemon juice and water. Cook, stirring continuously until thickened, about 5 minutes. Remove from heat and stir in the walnuts. Cool completely.

To assemble:
Roll out dough, half at a time, between two sheets of wax paper to form an 11x7-inch rectangle. Spread each rectangle with half of the filling. From wide end, roll up rectangles tightly. Wrap each in wax paper and chill until firm, about two hours or overnight.

Preheat oven to 375°. Butter baking sheets.

Slice cookies 1/4 inch thick. Arrange 1 inch apart on baking sheets. Bake until golden, about 8 to 10 minutes.

72 cookies

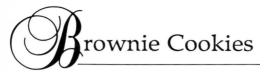rownie Cookies

a 12-ounce package semi-sweet chocolate chips	1 cup plus 2 tablespoons sugar
1 ounce unsweetened chocolate	1 teaspoon vanilla
2 tablespoons unsalted butter	1/2 cup plus 2 tablespoons flour
3 eggs	1/2 teaspoon baking powder

Preheat oven to 350°.

In top of a double boiler melt the chocolate and the butter. Remove from heat and cool to room temperature.

In a large bowl beat the eggs until foamy. Add the sugar, 2 tablespoons at a time, while continuing to beat, until the mixture is light and fluffy, about 2 minutes. Blend in the vanilla and chocolate mixture. Combine the flour and baking powder and mix well with the chocolate mixture.

Drop dough by rounded teaspoons onto two ungreased baking sheets. Bake until the cookies are just set, about 8 to 10 minutes. Do not overbake.

Remove from the oven and cool for 5 minutes. Transfer the cookies to a wire rack with a spatula.

36 cookies

int Chocolate Chip Cookies

4 egg whites, room temperature	12 ounces semi-sweet chocolate
1/8 teaspoon cream of tartar	chips
1 1/3 cups sugar	1/2 teaspoon peppermint flavoring
	6 drops green food coloring

Preheat oven to 350°. Line baking sheets with parchment paper.

In a mixer bowl beat the egg whites until stiff. Add the cream of tartar and gradually add the sugar, beating continuously. Beat for 2 minutes longer after all the sugar is added for a smoother texture. Fold in the chocolate chips, peppermint flavoring and coloring. Drop by teaspoonfuls onto baking sheets.

Set baking sheets in the oven. Turn oven off. Leave cookies in oven overnight.

Orange Chocolate Chip Cookies
Substitute 4 teaspoons grated orange rind and 1 1/3 teaspoons vanilla for the peppermint flavoring and coloring.

60 cookies

range Cookies

8 tablespoons (1 stick) unsalted
   butter
1 egg
1 cup sugar
1/2 cup sour cream
2 scant teaspoons baking powder

2 scant teaspoons baking soda
2 cups flour
pinch of salt
grated rind of 1/2 orange
Orange Frosting

Preheat oven to 350°. Butter baking sheets.

In a mixer bowl cream the butter and sugar well. Add the egg and beat until light and fluffy. Mix in the remaining ingredients. Drop by teaspoonfuls onto baking sheets.
Bake until brown at edges, about 8 to 10 minutes.
Cool slightly and frost with Orange Frosting. Let frosting dry well before storing cookies in airtight container.

Orange Frosting
juice of 1/2 orange
2 tablespoons unsalted butter,
   melted

confectioners' sugar

Mix orange juice and butter with enough confectioners' sugar to make the frosting of spreading consistency.

48 cookies

Frosted Chocolate Drops

2 1/2 squares unsweetened chocolate
8 tablespoons (1 stick) unsalted
  butter, softened
1 cup sugar
1 egg
1/2 cup half and half

1/2 teaspoon vanilla
1 1/2 cups flour
1 teaspoon baking soda
1 cup chopped walnuts or pecans
Chocolate Frosting

Preheat oven to 350°. Butter baking sheets.

Melt the chocolate in top of a double boiler. Keep warm.
In a mixer bowl cream together the butter and sugar.
In another bowl beat the egg and half and half with the vanilla.
Add to the butter mixture blending well.
Combine the flour and baking soda and add to the butter mixture. Stir in the melted chocolate and walnuts. (The batter should be thick so that it doesn't spread while baking.) Drop by teaspoonfuls onto prepared baking sheets. Bake for 12 minutes.
Cool and frost generously with Chocolate Frosting.

Chocolate Frosting
2 tablespoons unsalted butter
2 cups confectioners' sugar

3 tablespoons Dutch process cocoa
hot water

In a saucepan melt the butter and stir in the sugar and cocoa. Thin frosting carefully with the hot water, a tablespoon at a time, until it is of thick spreading consistency.

50 cookies

$\mathcal{C}$oconut Bars

1 cup flour
1/2 cup brown sugar

8 tablespoons (1 stick) unsalted
butter

Preheat oven to 350°. Butter a 9x9-inch baking pan.

In a mixer bowl combine the flour and sugar. Blend in the butter until mixture resembles coarse meal. Press lightly onto bottom of prepared pan. Bake until lightly browned, about 10 to 12 minutes.
Spread Coconut Topping on pastry. Bake 25 to 30 minutes.
Cut into bars when completely cool.

Coconut Topping
2 eggs
1 cup brown sugar
2 tablespoons flour
1/2 teaspoon baking powder

1/4 teaspoon salt
1 teaspoon vanilla
1 cup coconut
1/2 cup finely chopped walnuts

In a mixer bowl beat the eggs until light. Add the sugar, flour, baking powder and salt and mix well. Stir in the vanilla, coconut and walnuts.

20 bars

arrot Cookies

1 cup finely grated carrots
1 cup rolled oats
1 cup seedless raisins
1 cup chocolate chips
1/2 cup chopped walnuts
1 cup firmly packed brown sugar
2 cups flour
1 teaspoon baking powder

1/4 teaspoon baking soda
1/2 teaspoon cinnamon
1/2 teaspoon nutmeg
2 eggs, well beaten
1/3 cup milk
8 tablespoons (1 stick) unsalted
    butter, melted and cooled

Preheat oven to 350°. Butter two baking sheets.

In a large bowl mix together the carrots, oats, raisins, chocolate chips, walnuts and brown sugar.

In another bowl combine the flour, baking powder, baking soda, cinnamon and nutmeg. Blend thoroughly with carrot mixture.

In a separate bowl mix the eggs, milk and butter and stir into the carrot mixture. Dough will be stiff.

Drop by teaspoonfuls onto baking sheets. Shape and flatten cookies. Bake for 12 to 15 minutes.

50 cookies

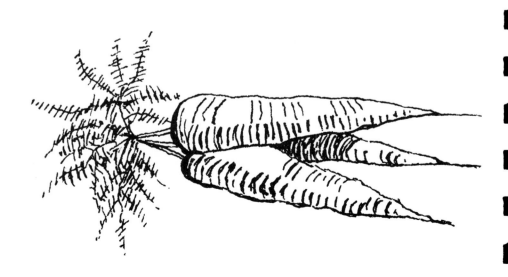

ACKNOWLEDGMENTS

The Cookbook Committee wishes to thank the League members who
contributed and tested recipes for DINING IN.

Lucy B. Ackemann
Evi Allen
Kathy Alward
Linda Amos
Joyce Barnhart
Shawna D. Barrett
Melanie Bell
Jeanie Bennett
Pegi Bernard
Liz Blasko
Pat Blaufuss
Jean Bleyle
Elisabeth K. Boas
Christa Boden
Tanis Bond
Belinda Bralver
Claudia Brandon
Barbara Breuer
Mary Lana Brown
Barbara Bruderman
Priscilla Bunn
Susan Smith Burns
Carol Carter
Meg Chappa
Colleen Charlesworth
Katie Chase
Patsy Cimarosa
Jane Cirino
Michele T. Cirino
Linda Clair
Carol Clukies
Carla Cohn
Ginny Colburn
Rose Marie Colletti
Mary Condon
Karen Connelly
Doris Cramer
Joan D'Andrea
Mary Dauman
Elizabeth DeAmicis
Ginger Donaher
Elizabeth A. Donahue
Barbara Karis Downey
Jane Draper
Anne Driver
Mikki Durishin-Williams

Beverly Ellsley
Sydney Emerson
Charlene Erwin
Francine Fass
Claudia Fenton
Daisy Fischtrom
Penny Fishman
Cindy Fitzgerald
Mari Fleming
Jane Forbes
Maryann Ford
Trudy Freeman
Sharon Frey
Sonja Friedman
Jacquelyn Fuchs
Belle Hilles Gadomski
Judy Gadzik
Sue Galati
Marie Garofalo
Carlotta Gladding
Connie Goodman
Patti Graebner
Colleen Grant
Karen Greenbaum
Mimi Greenlee
Nancy Hahnfeldt
Gerd Hammarskjold
Carol Hanks
Anne Harris
Barbara Hauer
Linde Healey
Marilyn C. Heffers
Susie Heintzelman
Candace Herbst
Ronnie Hittson
Jane M. Horton
Christina Jezierski
Carol C. Johnson
Jan Jones
Anne Fleming Juliano
Renie Karazin
Kathy Kincaid
•Lynn Kirsch
Kathryn Knapp
Mary Kneisel
Eileen Knittel

Maureen Kowall
Virginia Kress
Elizabeth Kuechenmeister
Kim Leonard
Kaye Leong
Ally Lerch
Karen Lessler
Barbara Levine
Karen Shaffer Levy
Elizabeth Lewis
Susan Littman
Maureen Luby
Alison Lundberg
Beverly MacGregor
Carole Malone
Marianna Marden
Cia Marion
Pat Markham
Barbara McGrath
Ellen McNees
Celeste McShane
Kathie Mermey
Alix Morin
Debbie Murphy
Maureen Myers
Kay Neal
Jean Neisius
Judy Nelson
Joy Neubert
Katie Nowlin
Judy O'Brien
Maureen Olson
Joyce Orkand
Dorothy Packer
Reggie Pape
Nancy S. Perrin
Tammy Pincavage
Janet Plotkin
Eunice Polito
Janet Preston
Kay Prybylski
Barbara Ramistella
Susan Reilly

Barbara Riley
Carole Rogers
Dorothy Rolla
Susan Jane Roots
Eva Rosenblatt
Terri Rotondo
Kandy Rowan
Susi Rubenstein
Sandy Rusher
Alma B. Ryan
Rose Mary Ryan
Marylea Schmidt
Patrice Schramm
Diane Schrier
Sharon Schroeder
Marian Schwartz
Susan Shuck
Carla Siegel
Carol A. Smith
Kay Smith
Patricia Smith
Stephanie Sorley
Denise Stehney
Linda Stern
Bobbe Sticklor
Liz Stokes
Harriet Stone
Judy Swann
Jeannette Tewey
Michele Thain
Nancy Tillson
Cheryl VanNess
Nan Wachen
Pamela Waesche
Terry Walsh
Ellen R. Wegert
Meryl Weight
Patricia Wieser
Terry Wilson
Charlotte Wilzbach
Claire Yearwood
Amy Zipkin

We are also grateful to League friends and relatives.

Marjorie M. Boas
Chris Condon
Eileen Dougherty
Mary E. Gates
Betty Havice
Jack Hittson

Marion Hittson
Inez Jerrett
Muriel Kaye
Joanne Knittel
Jacqueline Pearl
Jean Pepino

Mary Radison
Becky Rodgers
Angela Rolla
Carol Sherck
Kelly Sherck
Kerry Sherck

DINING IN
The Westport Young Woman's League
10 Bay Street, Suite 87
Westport, Connecticut 06880

Please send me _____ copies of DINING IN at $18.95 each $_____
Postage and handling at $2.00 each $_____
Connecticut residents add sales tax at $1.42 each $_____
Total Enclosed $_____

Please make check or money order payable to
The Westport Young Woman's League

Name _____ Charge to my Master Card ___

Address _____   Visa ___

City _____ Number _____

                                 Exp. Date _____

State _____ Zip _____ Signature _____

DINING IN
The Westport Young Woman's League
10 Bay Street, Suite 87
Westport, Connecticut 06880

Please send me _____ copies of DINING IN at $18.95 each $_____
Postage and handling at $2.00 each $_____
Connecticut residents add sales tax at $1.42 each $_____
Total Enclosed $_____

Please make check or money order payable to
The Westport Young Woman's League

Name _____ Charge to my Master Card ___

Address _____   Visa ___

City _____ Number _____

                                 Exp. Date _____

State _____ Zip _____ Signature _____

DINING IN
The Westport Young Woman's League
10 Bay Street, Suite 87
Westport, Connecticut 06880

- -

DINING IN
The Westport Young Woman's League
10 Bay Street, Suite 87
Westport, Connecticut 06880

COOK AHEAD PARTY DINNER

I

II

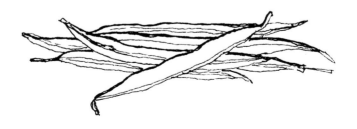

A WEEKDAY BREAKFAST ON THE RUN

TOMATO JUICE

SAVORY OMELETS   *page 57*

APPLE MUFFINS   *page 222*

BLUEBERRY MUFFINS   *page 222*

A LEISURELY WEEKEND BRUNCH

MIMOSAS

FRESH PINEAPPLE

CREPES WITH CHICKEN MUSHROOM FILLING   *page 66*
   OR

BAKED EGGS AND SAUSAGE   *page 58*

ASPARAGUS SPEARS   *page 64*

SCONES   *page 76*

PEACH CLAFOUTI   *page 79*

Westport is one of those proverbial commuter towns that short story and scriptwriters are so fond of depicting. The train station in this picture, one of two in town, is located in historic Greens Farms, founded in 1648 when settlers from nearby Norwalk and Fairfield decided to settle near the Saugatuck River and Long Island Sound.

Not too long ago, Westport onion farmers (for which the town was famous) sent their produce into New York City and neighboring towns on a daily basis. These days only a handful of local farms remain, and commuters to New York are often Westport Young Woman's League members who combine careers outside the home with family life.

271

273

275

LUNCHEON AL FRESCO

BACK COVER. *Westport is a major summer resort. Located along Long Island Sound and the Saugatuck River, summer activities include boating, canoeing, sunbathing and swimming, golf, tennis, horseback riding and polo, and just about any outdoor activity imaginable, including the old-fashioned game of croquet.*

What better way to take a break from an active summer's day than with a refreshing lunch in the garden.

A MEDITERRANEAN DINNER

By the sea, by the sea, by the beautiful sea is where you'll find many Westporters on a warm summer's day. From graceful sloops to sporty Catamarans, powerful cruisers or high speed racers, boating is a central activity in Westport. The Long Island Sound that borders the town is home to many public and private yacht clubs whose members enjoy the competition of a regatta. Yet for many, a short sail to nearby Cockenoe Island is challenge enough. This historic island is part of the nature preserve comprised of the numerous miniature islands that dot the Connecticut coastline. For Westporters, it's a favorite spot for tying up for a picnic or clambake, or simply to admire its natural beauty. But, whether it's a trip across the Sound to Long Island or simply a day of meandering off shore, most Westporters take their favorite summer foods aboard as they are sure to enjoy a meal along the way.